THE CLASSROOM CRUCIBLE

THE
CLASSROOM
CRUCIBLE

What Really Works,
What Doesn't,
and Why

EDWARD PAULY

BasicBooks
A Division of HarperCollinsPublishers

Library of Congress Cataloging-in-Publication Data
Pauly, Edward.
    The classroom crucible : what really works, what
doesn't, and why / Edward Pauly.
        p.   cm.
    Includes bibliographical references and index.
    ISBN 0–465–01150–0 (cloth)
    ISBN 0–465–01151–9 (paper)
    1. Classroom environment—United States.   2. Teacher-
student relationships—United States.   3. Education and
state—United States.   4. Education—United States—
Aims and objectives.
I. Title.
LB1033.P38   1991
371.1'023—dc20   90-55591
                                                              CIP

Designed by Ellen Levine

92 93 94 95 NK/CW 9 8 7 6 5 4 3 2 1

CONTENTS

ACKNOWLEDGMENTS   vii

INTRODUCTION: In the Crucible   1

PART I
The Significance of Classroom Life
in Teaching and Learning

1 The Discovery of Classroom Differences   19

2 Surrounded and Vulnerable: The Realities of Daily
   Classroom Life   36

3 Power over Everyone Else: Interactions
   That Control Classrooms   50

4 Why Classrooms Differ: Classroom Membership
   and Classroom Evolution   75

5 How Schools Influence Their Classrooms   93

PART II
Why Education Policies Have Failed, and How They Can Succeed

6 Lessons from Bitter Experience: The Laws
   of Education Policy   109

7 Policies That Take Classrooms Seriously   138

8 The Newton Solution: What Parents and Teachers
   Can Do Now   170

9 Helping the System Fix Itself: Education Policy
   from the Point of View of Students, Teachers,
   and Parents   197

NOTES   211

INDEX   229

ACKNOWLEDGMENTS

IN an important sense, this book is the product of a group effort involving teachers, students, principals, and parents in schools across the United States. I am especially grateful to the teachers and school administrators whom I interviewed, and whose words and experiences are recorded, albeit anonymously, in this book. Schools in California, Connecticut, Massachusetts, New York, Pennsylvania, and Virginia were gracious hosts to my visits, and I thank them. I wish particularly to express my appreciation to the teachers and students of the High School in the Community in New Haven, Connecticut, where I spent many hours observing classes.

I am also happy to have an opportunity to record my intellectual debt to the colleagues and friends whose assistance enabled me to complete this book. Much of the work on this book was done while I was a faculty member at the Institution for Social and Policy Studies, at Yale University. It was there that Richard Murnane and I spent hours struggling to make sense of the education policy research literature; those discussions continue to this day, and they have greatly influenced my work. Seymour Sarason gave unstintingly of his time, contributing ideas that are present throughout this book. Other ISPS faculty members also strongly shaped the ideas in the chapters that follow; I am especially indebted to David K. Cohen, Judith Gruber, Charles E. Lindblom, Theodore Marmor, Carl Milofsky, Richard R. Nelson, John Simon, Evan Stark, and Janet Weiss. As a setting that fostered innovative work in the social sciences, ISPS had no peer, and I am grateful to its directors, Lindblom, Nelson, and Joseph LaPalombara, and its assistant director, Terry Eicher, for supporting my work. While at Yale, I also received a grant from the National Institute of Education that provided time and resources to work on the book.

When I was starting the project that led to this book, I benefited greatly from responses to early drafts from my students in Yale College and Yale's School of Organization and Management: Susan Learner Barr, Andy Perkins, James Aronoff, Sara Bedford, Susan Condon, George Esahak, Theresa Glennon, Lucy Haagen, Randi Roth, Reva Siegel, and Tamar Siff were provocative and insightful listeners and critics. Jo Beld Fraatz and Richard Smithey, with whom I worked when they were graduate students in Yale's Department of Political Science, also contributed significantly to my thinking. At an even earlier stage, while I was a policy analyst at the Rand Corporation, I benefited enormously from lengthy and intense conversations with Paul Berman and Milbrey Wallin McLaughlin.

My colleagues at Manpower Demonstration Research Corporation, particularly Judith Gueron and Barbara Goldman, made the final preparation of the manuscript possible. At MDRC, Michael Bangser, Judith Greissman, Rob Ivry, and

Kay Sherwood helped me improve the manuscript. Invaluable suggestions were made by Martin Kessler, my editor at Basic Books. I am also grateful for the assistance of two old friends, James Henderson and Raymond Ollwerther.

My mother, father, and sister are present in every line of this book. My gratitude to them goes beyond words.

This is a book of ideas, although it is based on a great deal of statistical and observational evidence. I have drawn on my own data analyses and observations of schools, along with those of many skilled researchers, for the evidence presented here. However, no one but the author can be held responsible for the ideas in this book.

In the Crucible

IN the 1980s, Americans realized that their schools were in trouble. The public's frustrations at school mediocrity, poor student performance, and outright failure—and at not knowing what to do—led to dozens of reform proposals and to increased political visibility for education issues, but so far, little has been done that seems likely to reverse the schools' decline. American education is failing, and the reforms and rhetoric aimed at salvaging it are based on ineffective, misdirected views of how schools work. This book makes a dramatic claim, supported by the most rigorous research on education policy: the way that policy makers, researchers, and even parents and teachers approach education policy issues is simply wrong. The book sets forth a new way of thinking about schools, and a new approach to improving them through education policies and direct action by parents and teachers.

The book argues that the success or failure of the schools

depends on daily life in classrooms. Although it may seem hard to believe, education policy research has paid little attention to the influence of classrooms on education. Instead, the search for ideas about how to improve our schools has focused on quick fixes; researchers looked for the best curriculum, the best textbook, the best instructional method, the best kind of teacher, in the hope that once found, these solutions would make the schools work better. But the quick fixes have turned out to be as flimsy and evanescent as gossamer. An enormous volume of education research has turned up no curriculum, teaching technique, or special school program that consistently improves students' school performance.*

What has been lost in the whirl of controversy surrounding education is any real sense of what actually happens in a school. If asked, most people would probably agree with the proposition that education is built out of the ordinary, daily efforts of teachers and students in their classrooms. But education policy research, obsessed with the search for solutions to be imposed upon the schools, has shown little interest in ordinary school life or ordinary people in schools. Teachers and students *are* ordinary; in the United States there are roughly two million teachers and forty million students, so it is inevitable that they resemble the rest of the population in many ways. These teachers and students do their work

---

*The results of education policy research have been summed up in the leading review of research, which concludes: "Research has not identified a variant of the existing system that is consistently related to students' educational outcomes." This striking conclusion is supported by the extensive literature on educational programs, experiments, and research. The conclusions of this rigorous review of research have not been contradicted by any major study conducted since its publication, and its findings remain in force. In 1990, a review of recent research concluded, "Despite a vast amount of research conducted by very competent researchers, it is difficult to point with assurance to specific policies and programs that we can have confidence will have major substantive impact on student achievement across the wide range of very diverse high schools in the United States."[1] The statement is equally true for elementary schools.

behind closed classroom doors, most of the time without monitoring or supervision from higher-ups. Out of necessity, they are forced to learn how to be independent in the demanding work of teaching and learning.

This independence makes many school officials and policy makers very uncomfortable. Their response has been to focus their attention on school policies that they can control: official curricula, approved methods of instruction, and regulations governing who can teach. Education researchers, too, have put most of their energies into studying these kinds of issues. Obviously such issues matter; but they matter only indirectly, by affecting the daily lives of teachers and students, rather than by directly helping students to learn. The specific, individual problems of ordinary teachers and students in the classroom have been ignored, as if they were irrelevant to the question of how to improve education.

This book challenges this long-established tradition in education policy research. It begins with the idea that the lives and experiences of ordinary teachers and students must form the center of any serious analysis of efforts to improve our schools. Teachers and students are crucial to the success of the schools for several obvious reasons: because there are so many of them; because for the greatest part of every school day they are left to do their difficult work by themselves; and because in the end, the success of teaching and learning depends on what they do. This is no less true of the children of the poor than of other children. They and their teachers face the same daily task, as do all other students and teachers; they all must go into their classrooms each day and get on with their work.

This book concentrates on the shared settings that teachers and students face: the classroom, classmates, and the long school day repeated five times a week for forty weeks, year after year. It emphasizes the ways that teachers and students actually go about their work, rather than the ways in which they are *supposed* to go about it according to the official policies, rules, methods, and special programs that have been the focus of most education policy research. Finally, the book argues that education policies must respond to the particular situation in each individual classroom. This may seem a heresy to every proponent of the search for the "one best system" of education,[2] but in fact, the book's approach follows the oldest path of empirical social science. It describes what actually happens, rather than assuming that people's behavior always conforms to official policies; it examines past policies according to their effects rather than their rhetoric; and it analyzes the effects of people's daily behavior on the institutions in which they live and work.

The argument presented here is a simple one. The classroom is the crucible in which education takes place. The classroom holds the raw materials of education: the teachers and students; the materials for teaching and learning; the concentrated time for work; and the shared energy that comes from intense, sustained involvement with other people. Over the course of the school year, these raw materials are transformed by the heat and pressure of classroom life into a new amalgam of cooperation, conflict, and daily work. The classroom crucible is capable of producing extraordinary educational growth and success. It is also capable of producing disappointment and failure. The difference arises in the classrooms themselves, through the accretion of the actions that teachers, students, parents, school officials, and policy makers take in those classrooms. While these ideas about the critical importance of classrooms for education may not at first seem startling, later chapters will show that they represent a new and different way of thinking about how education works.

The people with the greatest stake in classrooms are those whose lives are directly affected by the quality of each day's classroom events: teachers and students. They are in the crucible. The ideas in this book provide intellectual backing for their sense of the importance of their classrooms, and for their struggles to teach and learn; it argues for education policies that will suport their work in the classroom crucible.

I began this book as an analyst of education policies. As I gradually thought through the essentially pessimistic conclusions of research on the many education policies that have been tried and found wanting, and when my own research produced similarly pessimistic results, I began to search for more fruitful ways of thinking about education. I visited schools; I sat in the backs of classrooms and watched students and teachers. I interviewed teachers, students, parents, and school officials. I thought about my own schooling in the then-recently desegregated public schools of Fairfax County, Virginia. I came to believe that education policies could only properly be understood as part of a broader picture of education, one solidly based on the realities of daily life in classrooms.

As I observed classrooms from kindergarten through high school, I also read the work of other researchers who were making important discoveries about the ordinary, day-to-day behavior of teachers and students in classrooms.* Their work was not focused on education policies, but instead concen-

---

*The first important book that I encountered on the connections between teachers' and students' behavior and the fate of education policies was Seymour B. Sarason, *The Culture of the School and the Problem of Change*. Other major works that analyze teachers' and students' classroom behavior include Philip W. Jackson, *Life in Classrooms*, and Dan C. Lortie, *Schoolteacher: A Sociological Study*, although these two excellent books do not emphasize teachers' and students' responses to education policies. I was also greatly influenced by Joseph Featherstone's brilliant and provocative review essay on *Schooling in Capitalist America* by Samuel Bowles and Herbert Gintis.[3]

trated specifically on the ways people behave in classrooms. Throughout its history, education policy research has seen teachers and students as passive, unresponsive followers who must be told what to do at every turn; but the research of the psychologist Seymour Sarason and others clearly shows that teachers and students are active, resourceful, and thoroughly involved in shaping their classrooms, sometimes with good results, and sometimes not. As I read their work, my own observations of classroom life began to seem more interesting and potentially significant. If teachers and students were active participants in the shaping of their work, then it was also possible that they might be affecting the policies that were supposed to be improving the schools. Gradually, I began to rethink the failure of education policies, and to make connections between the daily realities of classroom life and the capacity of policies to improve students' educational achievement. This book is the result of that process.

Casualties of the Debate on Education Policy

In order to see why the importance of classrooms has been ignored in the policy debate, some background and history are necessary.

We all are former students, and we carry our memories of school with us into adult life. The vigorous public debate over how schools should be run draws its energy at least in part from the intensity of these remembered school experiences. Every classroom accomplishment—a high grade, recognition from the teacher, success in a competition—and every failure—a wrong answer, a low grade, a humiliating rejection by one's peers—leaves its emotional imprint on us. Classroom experiences are deeply intertwined with students' developing personalities, and their nascent views of the world around them. As the years pass, the emotions that we carry with us from our former lives in school slowly are turned into our adult views on education policy—views about bilingual education, busing, required courses, achievement standards, and teachers' salaries.

Too often, our policy views have caused us to lose track of how our classrooms affected us. Making matters worse, the policy debate evokes the *emotions* tied to our old classroom experiences, without reminding us of the *reasons* those classrooms were important to us: the persistent and concrete daily presence of our teachers, our classmates, and the work we did together. That awareness of classroom experiences as the central part of schooling has been the chief casualty of the debate on education policy.

Of course, the education policy debate does more than just tickle the old emotions that surround our memories of school; it takes those emotions and builds them into powerful and provocative metaphors that have become the thirty-second sound bites of education. These have taken two main forms: the metaphor of control, and the metaphor of nurturance. Both control and nurturance have been used to shift the public's attention away from the daily classroom experiences of teachers and students, toward political platforms whose goal it is to elect one party or the other. Neither metaphor takes account of the diverse reality of classrooms—or classroom problems.

Instead, the metaphors tie education policy to two contrasting visions of school life. The control metaphor suggests that students are undisciplined, and that teachers often are incompetent and lazy. People who remember life in school as being about the struggle for control, or who fear the loss of control in schools or in society, logically will turn to proposals that emphasize tightened requirements for students and teachers and stricter enforcement of school rules.[4] These proponents of stricter controls seek to put teachers and students to work on a clearly defined curriculum, with strong supervision to see that they do their prescribed work. Among the recent proposals based on the metaphor of control are the demands for increased course requirements for students, increased testing of teachers and students, and toughened certification requirements and merit pay for teachers. Individual classrooms and their varied needs receive little attention here.

On the other side of the education debate are the proponents of nurturance. People who remember receiving (or wanting) caring treatment in their classrooms, and who see students as needing nurturing in order to learn, tend to favor policies that promise to take better care of students by providing better services, counseling, instructional materials, teacher training, and extra remedial instruction for low-achieving students. In practice, nurturance requires money—to pay for more expensive methods of instruction, and for higher salaries to attract good teachers.[5] But even these policies give scant attention to the breadth of problems that teachers and students confront in their classrooms; the money and the policies, not the classrooms, are the focus of attention.

The metaphors of control and nurturance have been used to support highly specific policies on teaching methods, textbooks, instructional materials, and testing. These policies are now the only ones that are seriously discussed, and they govern the ways that teachers are supervised, evaluated, and rewarded; the courses that students are required to take; the standards of school discipline; the programs in which low-achieving students are placed; and the ways in which money can be spent in the schools. The emotional metaphors of control and nurturance have come to dominate not only the education policy debate, but also the policies that are applied to the schools.

Consider the impassioned national debate over bilingual education for students whose native language is not English. The supporters of bilingualism argue that it nurtures non–English speakers as they make the difficult transition to a new language. Opponents of bilingualism assert that these students need to undergo the discipline imposed by complete immersion in English. Neither side of this debate over the symbolism of bilingualism versus English immersion is concerned about how these policies affect real classrooms. Both sides ignore the possibility that both bilingualism and English immersion can be well or badly taught; that they can help some students and harm others; that they can be used effectively by some teachers and not by others; and that they are therefore likely to succeed in some classrooms, but fail in others in the same school. These are the *classroom* issues that have been absent from the debate.

As this sterile debate continues, policy makers and citizens are taught the false lesson that bilingual education—and every other educational issue—can be reduced to two emotion-laden metaphors: that choosing a policy means choosing nurturance or control. Another false lesson implicit in the debate is that classrooms and classroom problems are not important. As we shall see, the lack of classroom-oriented policies has undermined both bilingual education and English immersion. Policy changes are described in part II of this book that escape the polarization of the debate, while suggesting ways to help both approaches succeed.

The political polarization of the education debate has tended to mask the fact that most voters accept both of education's emotional metaphors: they want tighter controls on the schools, *and* more money for them. Not surprisingly, that is what the government, in all its layers from local school districts to Washington, has provided: a flow of education policies that includes both controls and money.

The mixture of controls and money in education policy, and the absence of classrooms and their problems from the policy debate, has a long and significant history, reaching back to the nineteenth century. By 1840, the urban public-school movement was pushing for money to build and operate hundreds of new schools, and its supporters sought broad support by promising policies that controlled both students and teachers. The poor and seemingly unruly children of immigrants were to be Americanized, with large doses of indoctrination and demands for strict obedience;[6] teachers were to be closely supervised. At the same time, the schools spent huge amounts on teachers' salaries and new school buildings.[7] One side of the debate sought money and new schools; the other wanted tight controls. They both got what they wanted. Neither side paid any attention to classrooms and their problems.

At the turn of the century, financial crises in the cities led to deals between politicians and the business community which linked business support for increased education spending to increased controls on the schools. Business leaders agreed to support higher school taxes, so long as the schools accepted controls on what students were taught and maintained strict supervision of teachers' and students' work. Again, education policies were built from a combination of money and control, while ignoring classrooms. " 'Progressive' school superintendents found . . . businessmen their natural allies in reform," writes historian David Tyack. "Public school managers often catered to the wishes of their 'major stockholders,' the business leaders, especially with regard to vocational education and citizenship training. Civic-minded elites such as the Chamber of Commerce of Cleveland supported programs to build new schools, to improve public health, and to create playgrounds and vacation schools."[8]

In the early twentieth century, the progressive education movement popularized the idea of responding to students' needs and nurturing their growth. In practice, however, the progressives' reforms included not only new methods of instruction, but new controls as well: standardized tests for students, strict supervision for teachers, and in the words of the historian Lawrence Cremin, the introduction of "systematically organized and rational approaches to the administration and management of the schools."[9] Again, the emphasis was on more money and more controls, rather than on classrooms and solutions to classroom problems.

The present education policy debate differs little from this long-established pattern. The latest round of school reforms provides more money for teachers' salaries and additional services for students who are "at risk of failure," thereby gaining the support of the liberal camp. At the same time, the reforms have many conservative allies who support new curriculum requirements, graduation requirements, and tests to monitor both students and teachers.[10] The emotional metaphors of control and money continue to dominate the American education policy debate, and education policies continue to provide both of them.[11]

One more observation about the education policy debate can perhaps sum up the perversity of its hold on our thinking. In its present form, the education policy debate is essentially unresolvable, because its central premises can never be clearly tested against experience. Each time we discover that an effort to improve education by providing more money for the schools has fallen short, all we have learned is that that particular use of money hasn't worked; advocates will be quick to point out other ways of nurturing students that can be tried in the hope of finally finding one that will succeed. Likewise, for every policy that tightens regulations and controls on schooling but fails to improve students' achievement, *other* controls remain to be tried. So long as we restrict our attention to policies based on money and control, our policy debate will stay narrow, circular, and unresolvable.

Worst of all, the debate is fixated on policies whose effects on education are at best weak and indirect. In the words of one of the most prominent economists of education, Eric Hanushek, "the available evidence suggests that there is no relationship between expenditures and the achievement of students and that such traditional remedies as reducing class size or hiring better trained teachers are unlikely to improve matters."[12] The evidence shows that changes in family size and the socioeconomic composition of the schools accounted for a considerable fraction of the changes in student achievement in the 1960s and 1970s; that graduation standards and minimum-competency testing for graduating seniors did not contribute to the modest improvement in achievement that began in 1974; and that the effects of most school-related factors on the trends were either negligible or at best merely "plausible" and "apparently small."[13] It may be possible for policies to improve students' educational achievement—but evidently not the policies that have been at the center of the public debate. There is a lesson in this sad story: when a problem is as intractable as the problems of the schools have been, it is likely that something important has been left out of our thinking. That something is the classroom and its influence on teaching and learning.

A Guide to this Book

The evidence and ideas in this book are drawn from research on both elementary schools and high schools. Obviously, schools serving children of different ages differ in many ways, but as the reader will see, there are widely shared classroom experiences that make a broad range of classrooms quite similar in several important ways. The interviews with teachers and administrators that provide many of the book's illustrations come from diverse settings: from elementary and high schools, from schools in six states, from urban and suburban communities, and from affluent and low-income settings.

Part I of the book presents the evidence for the central role of classrooms (and the interactions within classrooms) in education. While the classroom is not the only part of the education system that affects teaching and learning, it does so in ways that are uniquely direct and powerful. (The other parts of the education system achieve their effects indirectly, by influencing classrooms.*) This classroom-based analysis of education is one that readers will immediately recognize from their own schooling, as well as from their children's experiences; it shows how the give-and-take between teachers and students determines the daily work that gets done in each classroom. It is an analysis that brings education policy face-to-face with the realities of classroom life. It presents the radical argument that education is the result of working agreements that are hammered out by the people in each classroom, who determine the rules, the power relationships, and

---

*Rebecca Barr and Robert Dreeben have shown that each level of the school organization produces results that affect the next lower level. For example, the school district issues policies that affect the principal, who in turn affects teachers, who affect students.[14]

the kinds of teaching and learning that will take place there.

Part II of the book shows the significance of the classroom for education policies, and why, in particular, standardized school policies inevitably fail to improve classrooms. Classroom-focused policies, which have far greater prospects for success, are explained, as are the actions that parents and teachers can take to improve their children's classrooms without waiting for education policy makers to change their failed approaches.

In order for education policies actually to improve the schools, a new approach to policy thinking is needed. Part II lays out such an approach, which I call *pluralistic policy*. Pluralistic policy explicitly abandons the search for the one best method that will fix everything. Instead, it puts school officials and specialists at the service of teachers, students, and parents. Pluralistic policy is aimed at solving the particular problems that arise in individual classrooms, by tailoring policies to the people who need assistance. In some classrooms this will mean increased attention to discipline; in others, new instructional approaches; in still others, the reassignment of students or teachers to more appropriate classrooms. This approach—well known to many school principals who have learned not to talk about it lest they be seen as rebels against school district policies—creates policies that fit the needs of the people in each particular classroom. The pluralistic policy approach also has important implications for teacher hiring, for the placement of teachers and students, and for making school and classroom choices available to teachers, parents, and students. Part II describes in detail a set of policies that take classrooms seriously, policies that base their effort to improve education on concrete measures to strengthen the daily work of teachers and students.

An important part of the problem of improving the schools

may be perceptual: we must learn to look at education policies from the point of view of students and teachers. Once we stop assuming that education is something that happens when teachers and students mechanically follow fixed policies, we will be able to see education being shaped by the active choices of teachers, students, and parents. Instead of relying on policies that ignore those choices, we can design policies that build on them. Instead of dutifully waiting for massive reform programs to work, we can act as parents and teachers to strengthen individual classrooms in our schools.

There always have been controversies in education. Sadly, the current controversies over education policy have little to do with the things that make one classroom more successful than another. The goal of this book is to show parents, teachers, school officials and policy makers new and powerful ways to think about education by thinking about classrooms.

One high-school history teacher summed up her view of the problems facing education policy:

> Policies that take classrooms seriously would be ones that account for the fact that learning takes place in the classroom, and that you can't implement a policy and just hand it down and assume that it's going to succeed in every classroom, or even assume that every teacher will use it. As soon as teachers shut the door we do what we want—Take account of *that*.
>
> A decent policy would totally reverse the way things are done now; they would come to the teachers and say, "What do you need?" I've never had anyone ask me what I need to be able to teach better. . . . It would be nice if there were services set up out there to serve the classroom, rather than people out there trying to figure out why things are going wrong in my classroom. I can tell you why things go wrong in my classroom! But when I list the things I need, there's no one to listen.

Policies that take classrooms seriously would be a whole new way of looking at the way schools work. Some of the talk about reform now is about this school-based management stuff, but still, it's *school*-based management; it's all based on the idea that we've just got to get a principal we can trust, and he can control all those lousy teachers. So they're still a step away from the classsroom; they're still really nervous about the idea of going down one more level, to the classroom. I think they don't *care* what's going on in the classrooms, as long as they don't hear it in the halls. So you would have to change the power structure so that the teachers and the students were the ones who were able to shape what was going on.

PART I

The Significance
of Classroom Life
in Teaching and Learning

CHAPTER 1

The Discovery
of Classroom Differences

FOR more than two decades, hard evidence has been mounting that challenges the basic assumptions of prevailing education policies, those favored by liberals as well as those favored by conservatives. This chapter describes the gradual, step-by-step discovery that classroom differences strongly affect student achievement, and that education policies have, by comparison, little to do with achievement differences. Researchers closely examined students' scores on standardized tests, systematically comparing the achievement of thousands of students in a wide variety of schools, educational programs, types of instruction, and policy regimes. Taken together, these studies reveal little difference in how much students learn as a result of one method of instruction rather than another. Astonishingly, the test-score evidence fails to support the achievement-boosting claims of *any* of the most publicized education policies. Even more important, the test-score studies demonstrate an incontrovertible connection between what students learn and the particular classrooms in which they work.

The Coleman Report

The critique of conventional education policies began in 1966, when the sociologist James S. Coleman and his colleagues published their analysis of the national survey of schools that Congress had commissioned two years earlier. Their report, *Equality of Educational Opportunity* (commonly referred to as the Coleman report), described the gap between white students' test scores and the much lower scores of black and Hispanic students.[1] They also reported that the school resources (teachers, money, books, and so on) available to white, black, and Hispanic students were approximately equal within each of the large regions of the country. The student/teacher ratio, for example, was almost the same for white and black students who attended school in a given region.[2] Coleman's evidence—that even when white students and black students received similar school resources, their test scores were far apart—inevitably raised the question of whether school resources had any effect on student achievement. School resources are a principal expression of education policies; if resource differences were found to have no direct effect on achievement, the whole structure of education policies would be thrown into question.

To find out whether or not school resources (and thus policies) were actually affecting achievement, Coleman looked for clues in the pattern of students' test scores. He used a statistical technique known as *analysis of variance* to weigh two competing explanations for the measured levels of the test scores.[3] One possible explanation emphasized the role of school resources and policies: it held that the differences between students' test scores were mostly due to differences between the schools that they attended. According to this view, some schools consistently out-performed others, thereby demonstrating that they had better educational policies and programs. If test scores were similar within each school, but greatly different from one school to another (which would be called *high variance due to schools*), it would follow that high-scoring schools must have more successful policies than low-scoring schools.* On the other hand, if there was a mixture of low and high test scores in each school, and most schools had an equally wide range of scores (a situation known as *low variance due to schools*), the implication would be that policy differences between schools had no consistent effect on student achievement. According to this view, some students in a school were doing well while others were doing badly, for reasons unrelated to the particular policy regime in their school.

There was no ambiguity about which view was supported by Coleman's data: the hypothesis that each school had highly varied student achievement turned out to be correct. Coleman found that "most of the variation in achievement could not possibly be accounted for by school differences, since most of it lies within the school."[5] As little as 10 percent of the variation in test scores was variance due to schools, while up to 90 percent of the variation occurred between students attending the same school. The evidence was clear: very little

---

*Of course, school-to-school differences in test scores could be caused either by differences in school policies, or by differences between schools in students' backgrounds. Coleman's analysis of variance separated these two sources of school differences.[4]

of student achievement depended on the school a student attended; and it followed that student achievement was not much affected by the policies imposed by their schools.*

To understand the significance of Coleman's findings, it is important to avoid misinterpreting his results. He did *not* find that schools had no effect on their students at all. In Coleman's study, all of the students were in school somewhere, and the fact that they were in school clearly had a great deal to do with their achievement. Students do not learn algebra by osmosis; they learn it by studying it in school.[7] What Coleman discovered was simply that no policy or program appeared to produce more knowledge of algebra than any other policy or program. Instead, student achievement appeared to depend on those things that varied within each school, such as students' home background, and their experiences in different classrooms in their school. Coleman's study challenged the underlying assumptions of conventional education policies by demonstrating that "vast inequalities in educational experience . . . exist inside schools."[8] These provocative words also sum up the many studies that followed and confirmed Coleman's findings.** The clear implication of Coleman's work is that something was happening within schools that was causing some students to have different ed-

*"School to school variations in achievement, from whatever source (community differences, variations in the average home background of the student body, or variations in school factors), are much smaller than individual variations within the school, at all grade levels, for all racial and ethnic groups."[6]

**In an important study by Rebecca Barr and Robert Dreeben conducted more than a decade after Coleman, researchers investigated fifteen first-grade classrooms in considerable detail: "Our evidence indicates that vast inequalities in educational experience—at least in first grade reading—exist inside schools and, to a lesser but by no means trivial degree, inside classrooms. . . . The inequalities appear to be of much smaller magnitude between schools." For example, in one school, the students identified as having the highest ability (the students in the top track) learned an average of 255 words in one classroom, while similar students in another classroom learned an average of 422 words.[9]

ucational experiences than others in the same school. And if students' experiences varied greatly within each school, virtually all of the efforts to improve education through generalized, schoolwide prescriptions were beside the point. Students were getting different educational experiences from schools that had been assumed to be giving them the same educational experience. What was causing this remarkable variation within schools?

By now, two decades after the Coleman report, everyone knows that there are large differences between the average test scores of students in poor, inner-city schools and those of students in affluent surburban schools. This achievement gap raises the obvious question of how Coleman could have found that differences between schools are not the source of differences in student achievement. Part of the answer is that Coleman did not find that all schools have the same average test scores; they don't. Student achievement has historically been strongly linked to family poverty; in schools with mostly poor students, average test scores have been quite low. What Coleman did find was that the wide dispersion of test scores within schools was not altered by extra school resources or other policies. Moreover, while the *average* test scores in middle-class schools were relatively high, students in those schools varied greatly in their scores: thus, there was no consistency in achievement, even among economically similar students exposed to the same policy regime in the same school. In poor communities, while the average scores were much lower, there was the same wide variation in achievement—and the same lack of any consistent effect of the school's resources or policies on achievement. For rich and poor, most of the variation in student achievement occurred within schools, not between them, thus ruling out schoolwide policies as a principal cause of the differences in student achievement.[10]* Family economic status helps or hinders a student's achievement; school resources and policies (at least the ones studied by Coleman) do not.

Coleman wrote: "A reasonable conclusion is . . . that our schools have great uniformity insofar as their effect on the learning of pupils is concerned. The data suggest that variations in school quality are not highly related to variations in achievement of pupils."[12] What Coleman's cautious language means is that the sum of all the systematic differences between schools, including all the differences caused by school policies and resources, have little effect on how much students learn. Some students learn more than others, but not for reasons that are traceable to differences in school policies.

Before the Coleman report, the vast bulk of education research was based on the idea that some school policies and programs were better than others; the researchers' job was to separate the successful policies from the failures. They searched for the most effective policies among proposals that were already part of the policy debate. The argument among researchers was only about which policies—which controls or resources—were successful. The Coleman report showed that such policies might not exist. It suggested that the reason thousands of education studies had failed to identify and agree on policies that would improve student achievement was the underlying futility of their mission.

Coleman's findings were as devastating to policies advocating more control of the schools (by regulating curriculum, instructional methods, or teacher and student behavior) as

---

*The high variation in student achievement within schools is matched by high variation in students' educational attainment (their total years of schooling): "Just as with cognitive skills, there is much more inequality in the educational attainment of different students in the same high school than between the average student in one high school and the average student in another high school."[11]

they were to policies advocating more resources. At a time when schools were being desegregated, when school spending was increasing and many new programs were being tried out, the idea that school policies produced no consistent differences in student achievement seemed fatalistic, even destructive. Coleman recommended no new policies and made no suggestions for overcoming the problems he had identified; as a result, his work was attacked for undermining efforts to improve the schools.[13] Coleman responded by pointing out that his research method actually overestimated the effects of school policies, since his measures of school factors included the effects of the surrounding community and the average family background of students enrolled in each school.[14] The finding that some students did well and some did poorly, regardless of their school's policies, would not go away so easily.

Post-Coleman

When the entire literature of evaluation studies from the 1960s through the mid-1980s is taken together, one finds no known policies that consistently improve student achievement—which is exactly what Coleman found. In education research, most evaluation studies are relatively modest in scope; they examine the effects of a new curriculum or a new teaching method in a small number of classrooms and schools. Frequently, these small-scale studies find that the new curriculum or teaching method appears to work: in the small sample of students who have been exposed to the experiment, achievement goes up. Unhappily, what usually happens is that the same program, used in another school, fails to repeat the earlier success, and at the original site, the initial results typically fade away after a year or two.[15] These temporary, localized successes usually are attributed to the "Hawthorne effect": people tend to work harder when they think that they are part of a new and important experiment.* After the first bloom of success, their work returns to normal, and the initial gains in performance vanish.[16] Both the findings of the small-scale studies and Coleman's appeared to have brought education research to a dead end. But as often happens, one discovery triggered another. In 1969, a Harvard faculty seminar was convened to discuss Coleman's findings and to reanalyze his computerized data files. Since Coleman's use of statistical analysis was substantially more sophisticated than previous research on education, and since his methods had been vigorously criticized, no one knew what to expect from the seminar's reanalysis of the data. The results were presented in a five-hundred page book, *On Equality of Educational Opportunity,* edited by the great statistician Frederick Mosteller and then-professor Daniel Patrick Moynihan. Their conclusions strongly supported Coleman's main assertion: achievement differences were much larger within schools than between them.[17] Another result of the Harvard faculty seminar—one just as important as its conclusions—was a batch of new suggestions for how the next generation of researchers could grapple with the troubling implications about education policies that Coleman had forced upon everyone's attention.[18]

A young economist from the Massachusetts Institute of Technology named Eric Hanushek, who had been a co-author of one of the Harvard seminar papers,[19] discovered a way to turn the seminar's suggestions into a new study design. His

---

*The original research that is the basis for the widely known Hawthorne effect was done between 1924 and 1936 at Western Electric's Hawthorne works, outside of Chicago, by Fritz Roethlisberger and Elton Mayo, industrial psychologists, and William Dickson, a Western Electric engineer.

work built on the Coleman report, but went far beyond Coleman's work, and in the process made the crucial discovery about the role of classrooms in shaping student achievement. Hanushek opened up the possibility of a new approach to analyzing education, by casting off the blinders that had seemingly paralyzed research on education policy.

It was no accident that Hanushek found a solution to the problems raised by the Coleman report. His work on the Harvard reanalysis of Coleman's data had shown him the problematic statistical assumptions that he needed to avoid. His training in econometrics gave him access to a wide range of statistical ideas that were not part of conventional education research; and he had the imagination to see possibilities in statistical techniques that others had missed. By using more detailed information than previous researchers, and by starting with a simple, specific research question, he was able to untangle the central mystery in the Coleman report—the reason why school policies failed to affect students' achievement.

What Hanushek did was to abandon assumptions about the importance of schoolwide policies, and instead to explore why student test scores were so varied within each school. His insight was simple: If individual classrooms in a school were found to have dramatically different gains in student achievement, that would explain why there were large differences in students' test scores within that school.[20] Hanushek had realized that similar students (in family background, economic status, and prior school success) attending the same school might have different educational experiences simply because they were in different classrooms. If classrooms within the same school were different, then the search for successful education policies would have to change its focus from school policies to individual classrooms. Conversely, if there were no differences in the achievement gains of similar students in different classrooms in a school, then presumably some uniform school policy or program was at work in all of that school's classrooms. Hanushek saw that if he could design a statistical method that accurately measured student achievement gains in each classroom, he could compare the extent to which schoolwide policies, individual classrooms, and home background influenced student achievement.

The first question Hanushek needed to answer was whether there was a substantial difference in what a student learned over the course of a school year that depended on the classroom to which he or she belonged, and was not caused by the student's home background and previous school achievement. That finding would show for the first time whether in fact classrooms were different in their ability to educate a given student, or whether a student's achievement was determined by the policies and teaching methods in the student's school.

Results of the Classroom Studies

Hanushek's method used two test scores for each student: one measuring achievement at the beginning of the school year, and the other measuring achievement at the end of the year. The first score summed up the educational foundation possessed by each student at the beginning of a new school year: that student's prior learning, intelligence, and experiences at home and in the community. The second score could then show how much *additional* learning he or she added to that foundation over the course of the year. Because each student's measured gain in achievement would take place in one classroom during a single school year, it would reflect the educational effect of a single classroom, allowing Hanushek to compare the achievement gains that took place in different classrooms. (In most elementary schools, students are assigned to one classroom for the entire school year; in secondary schools, students are assigned to different classrooms for different courses. In both examples, however, instruction in a given subject takes place among a single body of people who share the same classroom. Thus, when the effect of a classroom on a student's achievement is measured, it includes the effect of everything that happens to a student in a given classroom over the course of the school year. In elementary classrooms, this includes the whole day's events; in high schools, it includes everything that happens in the hour-long English class, for example, every day for a year.) After locating a school district that had maintained the student and classroom data he needed, Hanushek finally was able to perform his analysis.

What he found was that there were substantial differences in how much students learned in different classrooms.[21] This was true even for students of the same age, race, family background, and economic status. It held true even for students who had started the school year with the same test scores: when Hanushek compared the learning gains of students whose initial scores were the same, the amount gained by these students was different in each classroom. Thus, each student's end-of-the-year test score depended on his or her classroom. No one had known about these striking classroom differences in student achievement until the Hanushek study—to look for them would have denied the importance of schoolwide education policies.

Achievement differences even existed between classrooms next door to each other in the same school. Hanushek found that in some classrooms students learned a great deal, even if their past performance hadn't been very good. In other classrooms, there was little progress, even for bright students; in still other classrooms, students made a middling amount of progress. If one thing was clear, it was that *classrooms mattered;* the students in a given classroom tended to make similar amounts of progress in what they learned.* Initially, Hanushek suggested that the explanation of why classrooms mattered might lie in the abilities of individual teachers; as we shall see, however, later evidence showed that whole classrooms, rather than consistently successful teachers, are the cause of achievement gains (see pp. 31–32 and chapter 4).

In 1972, Richard Murnane, a graduate student in economics at Yale, read Hanushek's first report on his student achievement research, and extended Hanushek's method to seven new samples of poor, inner-city students.[24] Subsequently, Murnane joined a research team evaluating the educational effects of welfare reform proposals, and used the opportunity to apply Hanushek's technique to four more samples of students.[25] In 1976, I used Hanushek's method to study the achievement of black and Hispanic students in Los Angeles.[26] Every sample confirmed the discovery of classroom differences in achievement: each classroom produced a distinctive level of student achievement, compared with all other classrooms. The differences held up for students in the first grade, the sixth grade, and grades in between; for whites, blacks, and Hispanics; in New England, California, and the Midwest; in test scores for reading, math, and even spelling.

*In Hanushek's initial research reports, he wrote that "different teachers and different classroom compositions do not affect the achievement outcome of Mexican-American students."[22] Subsequently, it became clear that there were too few Mexican-American students per classroom for statistical tests to measure their response to classroom differences. (In technical terms, the power of the statistical tests was insufficient to analyze the achievement of the Mexican-American students in his sample.) When larger numbers of Mexican-American students were studied using Hanushek's technique, the same results were obtained as for other groups.[23]

Most (but not all) of the students in these studies were poor—precisely those at whom the latest education policies were aimed; yet their achievement was clearly more sensitive to classroom differences than to policy differences. By 1979, Hanushek, Murnane, and I independently had analyzed test scores and classroom-achievement patterns for seventeen separate samples totaling more than 6,300 students: the first consistent pattern of rigorous research results in the long effort to explain why education policies failed to affect student achievement.

Our discovery documented an important and powerful truth: a student who attends a particular school is not educated in the whole school; he or she is educated in particular classrooms *within* that school. A school and its policies do not necessarily determine its students' educational experiences. The distinction between the school and its classrooms is crucial; teaching and learning take place in individual classrooms, which can easily differ from each other.

Interpreting the Evidence

At the time, however, the search for successful policies led us away from the implications of our discovery about classrooms. The new results were hard to grasp, so different were they from what we had expected to find. Existing education research gave us little help in understanding classroom differences, or in figuring out what produced them. We kept searching for effective policies, as did Coleman.

Continuing his work (in research not yet published), Murnane found that teachers who are successful with one classroom may not be successful with another, even if the students in the classrooms are similar. When he compared the achievement gains of different classes taught by the same teacher in two successive years (using Hanushek's rigorous statistical methods), he found only a very weak tendency for teachers to repeat their previous performances. This clearly implies that a teacher's effectiveness depends on the particular group of students in his or her classroom.[27] This finding suggests that policies based on rating or testing teachers' pedagogical skills are unlikely to serve as a useful basis for improving schools, because a teacher's skills have different effects in different classrooms.

My own research also focused on teaching methods as a possible source of classroom differences in achievement. The results were clear, and completely consistent with Hanushek's and Murnane's findings: a long list of policies and teaching methods was demonstrated to have no effect on student achievement. I collected a great deal of information on teachers' instructional methods, and carefully matched it with individual students' achievement gains. The findings showed that *classrooms* produced different levels of achievement, while no teaching method had a consistent effect on achievement. There were many successful inner-city classrooms included in the study, but all were doing things differently from each other.[28]

Ten years after their test score studies, both Eric Hanushek and Richard Murnane wrote articles reassessing their work. Unlike other education researchers, they had by then given up on the search for schoolwide policies that would raise student achievement. Instead, both researchers returned to their original discovery, now thoroughly confirmed, of classroom differences in student achievement. Murnane wrote,

What have we learned from quantitative studies of school effectiveness? The most notable finding is that there are significant differences in the amount of learning taking place in different schools and in different classrooms within the same school, even among inner-city schools, and even after taking into account the skills and backgrounds that children bring to school. The importance of this result, found in all [studies] that have addressed this question, cannot be overestimated.[29]

Hanushek forcefully reemphasized the fact that "differences in teacher performance cannot be described by any simple set of characteristics such as the backgrounds of teachers, classroom organizational techniques, presentational styles, and so forth."[30] Both new articles underscore the fact that when student test score gains are carefully examined, the important differences are between successful and unsuccessful classrooms, differences that cannot be traced to consistent school policies, characteristics or behaviors of teachers, curricula, teaching methods, or special programs.

Why has there not been a great deal of coverage of the discovery of classroom differences in student achievement—one of the very few rigorous, thoroughly confirmed findings to emerge from decades of education policy research? The answer is that in order for a body of research to be discussed, it must be understood and restated in the language of prior research. The Coleman report's finding of large achievement gaps between white and minority students was immediately understood and debated; it spoke directly to researchers' longstanding concerns. Coleman's (and Mosteller's) finding that most variation in achievement occurred within schools was far more difficult for researchers to comprehend and discuss; and Hanushek's discovery of classroom differences in achievement went even farther, entirely confounding existing ideas. If every classroom had its own distinct effect on achievement, then most education policy research would have to be replaced; but there was no new theory at hand that could explain the new result. Consequently, research could not readily take account of the classroom difference findings; and in fact, it did not.

The classroom-achievement-difference studies of the 1970s, along with other pathbreaking education policy research (particularly Harvey Averch's review of education policy research and the Change Agent study, discussed in chapter 6) have received far less attention than they merit. The early publication dates of these studies do not diminish their importance but heighten it; no equally rigorous studies since have contradicted their findings. The dramatic, consistent, and unrefuted results of these studies have paved the way for new interpretations.

The discovery of classroom differences in student achievement provides new grounds for optimism about schools. Instead of simply adding to the evidence that policies have failed, these studies show the underlying cause of the failure: education policies that depend on schoolwide prescriptions and uniform compliance from teachers and students, when the reality of schooling is that all classrooms are different. This discovery explains what all of the research on schoolwide, uniform policies has completely overlooked: the stories of individual teachers and classrooms that succeed without following prescribed policies.* The central question about

---

*The phenomenon of successful individual classrooms that deviate from their school's prescribed policies appears to account for the wildly inconsistent pattern of results in the evaluation literature. When an evaluator stumbles onto a school that happens to have one or two successful classrooms, these classrooms' test score gains can pull up the school's average enough to make the whole school and its policies appear to be succeeding. When the evaluation is repeated in another school with the same policies but without the successful classrooms, the result appears to contradict the earlier study. In both schools, the proportion of successful and unsuccessful *classrooms* determines the school's average test score gain and thus the result of the evaluation—although the evaluator assumes that each school's *policies* are responsible for the evaluation results.

schools should not be "Why doesn't anything work?" but "Why do some classrooms succeed, while others in the same school don't?" The optimism contained in this question provides the basis for a new approach to improving the schools, as later chapters of this book will show.

The discovery of classroom differences in student achievement has not yet succeeded in changing the education policy debate, because people still equate education policies with controls and resources. As a result, the market for conventional policies continues to flourish, despite the lack of evidence that they work. Alternative kinds of policies do not yet exist. Politicians and education officials need practical education policy proposals, and since the new evidence on classroom differences did not immediately provide new policy ideas, the old ideas continue to hold sway.

The discovery of classroom differences showed that classrooms and the people in them are at the core of successful schooling. The superintendent of an urban school district, known as an effective reformer and activist, put it this way:

> To expect that we can have principals or curriculum directors or even superintendents profoundly influence what goes on in the classroom—I think we're deluding ourselves. Principals and curriculum can be called in as resources, and can certainly serve some regulatory and statutory functions. But where it's going to happen—or not happen—is in the classroom, and within a peer network. The classroom, my god . . . it's a whole world right there. Sometimes I think that they are the ones who are really in charge of education.[31]

Many parents are likely to agree. They are, in this respect, far ahead of prevailing education policies.

CHAPTER 2

Surrounded and Vulnerable:
The Realities
of Daily Classroom Life

THE most important experiences of classroom life are shared by people in every kind of elementary- and secondary-school classroom, regardless of whether their school is urban or rural, affluent or poor. Coming to school every day, going to one's classroom, seeing the familiar faces there: these are the universals of classroom life for both students and teachers. Classroom life may sometimes be touched by education policies, but its foundations are the daily interactions among the people in each individual classroom. Teachers and students and their interactions are the raw materials of teaching and learning.

I interviewed teachers in inner-city and suburban schools in six states to find out how classroom experiences affected them and their students.* This is what teachers said about life in their classrooms:

---

*All teachers' and students' names are pseudonyms. Questions on numerous

You have to be *on,* always on, no matter whether you're tired or whatever. For those five periods a day, you have to be on. The number of human interactions you have are just phenomenal. And you're thinking about what you're teaching, and trying to gauge from them whether it's working, and seeing what Joanne Grant's doing in the back row, whether she's really harassing someone or whether it's a friendly thing going on—it's just an incredibly highly-demanding-of-concentration activity. I mean, I look at my husband's job and *maybe,* in the course of a day, he deals with ten people. And that's a big day. That's what I mean when I say that it's an intense activity.

Sometimes the worst things can happen, because of the effect that students can have on the other students, and on the teacher. You're so vulnerable. Sometimes it's too much. They affect each other's level of intensity. And that happens in all schools; it's got to happen. If I'm stumbling through a question, and my energy is going down, and they're invested enough in the issue at that point that they want to keep it going, then they'll do whatever they can. "I know!"—and then they give it to you, and they give it to each other. If they're not invested in it, then it falls apart.

The students come in, day after day after day. In some ways, their schedule is more relentless than ours; we have a period for prep and a period where you monitor study hall, which doesn't require that much work, and a lunch period— whereas they have seven classes. So they're trying to figure out a way to get through that kind of relentless pace.

These teachers are describing the unremitting intensity of life in the classroom, for both teachers and students. This is the

---

aspects of classroom life were asked and probed. The interviews were transcribed from tape recordings. When two or more quotations are grouped together, each quotation comes from a different respondent.

backdrop for everything that happens during the school day, and it underlies all of the relationships and interactions that make classrooms work.

Teachers and students work where they are always surrounded and vulnerable, held in the grip of unavoidable, enforced relationships between each person and all other members of the classroom. They spend their whole day working in classrooms made up of people who watch each other, respond to each other, and have the ability to make life productive and pleasant—or impossible—for everyone in the class. The classroom's members are surrounded, vulnerable, and exposed to each other—held together in the classroom crucible.

In his book *Life in Classrooms,* Philip Jackson writes:

> There is a social intimacy [in classrooms] . . . that is unmatched elsewhere in our society. Buses and movie theaters may be more crowded than classrooms, but people rarely stay in such densely populated settings for extended periods of time and while there, they usually are not expected to concentrate on work or to interact with each other. Even factory workers are not clustered as close together as students in a standard classroom. Indeed, imagine what would happen if a factory the size of a typical elementary school contained three or four hundred adult workers. In all likelihood the unions would not allow it. Only in schools do thirty or more people spend several hours each day literally side by side. Once we leave the classroom we seldom again are required to have contact with so many people for so long a time.[1]

Jackson sums up classroom life as "the daily grind."[2] The daily grind is the universal experience of classroom life: being surrounded, all day, every day, by a group of people who join in and closely watch your activities, your accomplishments, and your failures. Teachers describe the classroom experience as being one of intense pressure:

> They are there from eight o'clock in the morning until three forty-five, every day, every day, every day. It doesn't matter if you would rather see them at two o'clock. You're stuck. And you're also constantly bombarded with whatever is on the kids' agenda that day. Coupled with what's on your agenda—you may not be having a great day, and that kid may be having a rotten day—and then, fireworks! You're set up; you have no other alternative; you've got to interact with that kid.

> It's an unnatural way to have a day; in other professions, you may have meetings and that type of thing, but even if you have a meeting scheduled you can usually change it, if something goes wrong. But I always have twenty-five kids waiting for me.

> I'm always going from one [student] to the next. You go from one intense connection, to another, to another. You could go nuts doing this; you really could. With my sixth period class, I take a deep breath when they're getting ready to come in, because I know they're going to be a handful. And I have to be on top of it, I have to have slept well the night before, I can't be tired. You just can't get by without really *being there*.

> It's a public forum. It's like for a lawyer to be in court, on trial, *every day*. For the whole day. For the teacher and the taught [the students]. For the students, it's a pressure-cooker that they're in every day. For the teachers—[Pause]. That's one reason why it's such tiring work.

These descriptions clearly show that classrooms are not just places that happen to be full of people; they are places where everyone is constantly aware of the people around them, responding to and being deeply affected by them. This pattern of crowded, intense intimacy is the setting for daily life in classrooms.

My observation of elementary- and high-school classrooms has led me to identify three characteristics that combine to create the remarkable circumstances in which teachers and students work.

1. Each person in the classroom can affect how the others are treated. There is no teacher or student unable to gain the attention of his or her classmates and to impinge on their lives and work; and every person is at the mercy of the other people in the classroom.[3]

2. Teachers' and students' actions are continually exposed to examination by every person in the classroom, in an unrelenting mutual scrutiny that gradually reveals each person's sensitivities and limitations to everyone else in the classroom, and greatly increases their susceptibility to influence by their classmates.[4]

3. Teachers and students know that their contact with the other people in their classroom will be lengthy and sustained. For the whole school year, the quality of teachers' and students' lives is controlled by a single group of people, those that make up their classroom. They are always *there*.*

Taken together, these characteristics of classroom life shape all of the teaching and learning that takes place in school. What follows will show why each of them is so important.

---

*Seymour Sarason builds his description of the "classroom constitution" on the observation that people in a classroom realize they will be living and working together for a whole year.[5]

Each person's ability to affect how the others are treated

Students and teachers affect the people in their classroom by paying attention or withholding their attention, by being helpful or difficult, by caring about the concerns of others or rejecting them.[6] Because they work together in close quarters every day, every action taken by a teacher or student is, in effect, imposed upon the rest of the classroom. When a student disrupts the class, or when a teacher is slow to begin a lesson, everyone's work is affected. When students compete to answer questions, or when a teacher presents a stimulating and engaging assignment, the intensity of teaching and learning increases. Each time a student or teacher does something that undermines or devalues the work of teaching and learning, the others are likely to draw back from their involvement in that work.

Many teachers recognize how much they are affected by students, and they also see the ways in which students are affected by their classmates:

> You're always focusing on who's paying attention, who's listening, are they interested. That's constant. You need to have everybody paying attention. Because later, you can't remind them how to do their papers if you're busy working with another group. And if they're not listening, they won't know how to do it, and you don't have the time to tell them.

> There are sometimes children that can't sit on the rug and give you their attention. And they'll start bothering *other* people. And then *you* get involved.

> If somebody comes in in a bad mood—they've had a terrible bus ride, they've already punched out three people in the hallway before they got down to the room—that person

could turn the whole classroom upside down, and get everybody so keyed up that you can't do anything.

If they're just sitting around, or if they're not responding
to what I'm saying, it affects everything. I get jerks [in my
classroom]; teachers in the honors classes get them; all teachers get jerks. And in each class, they can be jerks in new
ways. It's the way they interact with each other. It affects
everything. There are things you can do in one class that you
can't do in another—and not because of the ability level.

There is no mistaking what these teachers are saying: what
works in their classrooms is determined by what their students do. Students decide how to respond to their teacher's
instructions, how to treat their teacher and their classmates,
how to respond to a distraction or a whispered comment, and
how hard to work. They have the ability to disrupt the class,
withdraw from it, or simply cease paying attention to what
is being taught. Their actions forcefully impinge on their
teacher's work, and on the work of their classmates.

Even young children have the ability to bring their classroom to a halt by having a tantrum. Older students can be
more subtle—noisily dropped books and carefully aimed
paper wads are well-known forms of disruption. Students can
direct their behavior at the whole class, or they can focus
on a single classmate by whispering comments, teasing, or
glaring.

As the students' behavior shapes each classroom, so too
does the teacher's behavior. Teachers influence their students
by handing out praise or punishment, giving or withholding
assistance, refereeing disputes or letting students loose on
each other. Like their students, teachers can try to influence
the whole class or a single troublesome student, or both—
as this example shows:

When there's a guy who has his hat down like this, and he's sitting back, and his face is cloudy, I can make a jocular comment—"Wow, there's this huge energy drain on this side of the room!"—and make all the other kids laugh, and it puts some pressure on the kid, but in a very specific way that's not at all shaming, it's just fun: "That's my energy drain over there." If there's one thing I have to definitely avoid, because it's a no-win situation, it's getting yourself in a little call-and-response with a student, where everyone is watching, judging; there's no way of winning, there's *no way*. Even if you become authoritative, and you get the student to sit down, you've *lost,* because nobody is going to listen to you. Sometimes that happens anyway; and you try to do everything in your power to avoid it.

When these classroom strategies work, they make teaching and learning possible; when they fail, they temporarily demolish the possibility of serious work. In both cases, they demonstrate the ability of teachers and students to affect the other people in their classroom. The success of teaching and learning depends on the willingness of the classroom's members to pay attention, cooperate, and treat each other reasonably well.

Mutual scrutiny

Classrooms are places where teachers' and students' actions are always open to view. There is no privacy in a classroom. Everything that everyone does is inspected by everyone else. Students and teachers may be strangers to each other in September, but they quickly get to know a great deal about each other, and about each other's soft spots as well.[7] Teachers report the effects of always being under observation, and always observing:

Once when we were doing critiquing [in a high school art class], they said they wanted to be me. I said, "Oh, fine; do it." And they got up and mimicked me: "I think they could balance the work a little bit better here," all the same ideas that I was using with them, the ideas about the elements of design. It was a scream. I had never realized how much was getting through; and it was. They were seeing it all.

The students are looking at you and you are looking at them. I gave a homework assignment the first week [of September]; the next day all the kids brought in the homework assignment except one, and I called her on it and immediately she was very apologetic and "Oh Miss Williams I'm very sorry," and she brought it in for me after school. But it was obvious that she was trying to figure out whether I was one of those teachers who assigned homework and never read it afterwards and never cared, or whether I really did care about the homework. And everybody else was watching to see what would happen.

You sit there, or walk around, and you just pick up signals from them. *All the time.*

They're finding out how you're going to treat them, and you're finding out how they're going to treat you.

They've got the scoop on you by the end of September. They know everything about that classroom, [because] they've been there since it started.

This experience of watchfulness and of always being watched lends an extra degree of gravity and intensity to teachers' and students' vulnerability in their classrooms. Their awareness of being scrutinized reminds them that their actions will be remembered by those who share their classroom.

The reason for the unending mutual scrutiny to which people in classrooms subject each other is a perfectly rational one: they are faced with great uncertainty about how others are going to treat them, so they watch for clues about the future behavior of those who surround them. Gradually, initial uncertainty is replaced by quite intimate knowledge, because close scrutiny exposes individual sensitivities. Whatever skill, ability, or characteristic a teacher or student is most insecure about will inevitably be seen and noted by other people in the classroom. People who are not part of a classroom can develop a self-protective veneer that hides their special sensitivities; because of their constant mutual scrutiny, people in classrooms have no such shield against the carefully-targeted demands and rejections that are an unavoidable part of classroom life.

An important consequence of mutual scrutiny in classrooms is that it keeps each person's attention closely fixed on those with whom they must work, as the teachers' stories show. By watching the people around them, teachers and students are able to interpret the significance of classroom events. When does a teacher or student really mean it when he or she asks for something? (Watch what happens when the request is ignored.) Who can be trusted? (Watch for betrayals and accusations, by both teachers and students.) Who is emotionally attached to whom? (Watch the classroom romances.)[8] The highly personalized information amassed by students and teachers about the people who surround them every day becomes a bank of knowledge on which they can draw when they need to know how someone is likely to behave. Moreover, this knowledge is continually replenished by each new day's mutual scrutiny. Even the youngest students watch and remember events in their classroom, and adjust their actions in response to what they have seen.[9]

Among the many things that teachers and students learn from their mutual scrutiny is the effectiveness of various efforts to teach and learn. When a teacher's presentation of new material leaves students confused, everyone notices, which strongly encourages the teacher to try some other, safer instructional approach. When a student does poorly in an oral assignment, that failure becomes a label; the student is less inclined to risk failure again, and more inclined to withdraw from learning. The result of mutual scrutiny is intense vulnerability for both teachers and students.

Lengthy and sustained contact

In ordinary life outside of schools, our dealings with others are typically brief and controllable. Meetings in shopping malls, casual conversations, and even many workplace and family encounters often are limited to the business at hand: a purchase, a question and its answer, or a request for a particular piece of work can be disposed of quickly. These relationships contain a kind of trial-and-error clause: if you don't like the way you are being treated, you can simply complete your business and leave. In classrooms, by contrast, teachers and students cannot simply complete their involvement with each other and then leave the arena; they must continue to work together. They are, in an important sense, stuck with each other.

The length of time spent with the other people in one's classroom means that seizing short-term advantages can be costly in the long run. People who are badly treated have lots of opportunities to get even. This inescapable fact makes everyone in the classroom vulnerable:

Since you're with the kids for a full year, once something happens, like a kid finds out he can really needle another kid by doing something in particular, once that happens—everybody has seen it, and you can't make it go away. It's permanent, because everybody will remember it until the end of the year.

You don't know what will happen—sometimes it has just blown up in my face. And then I say [to the students], "When you're in the classroom, this is your school family, and just like the people in your family, we have to live through a hundred and eighty-five days together, so why don't we make it the best that we can." And usually the kids grumble and gripe. But the more you plug at it, it usually ends up working out.

You can always wait them out. When things go wrong, you wait, because there will always be another chance to connect with that kid.

Classroom relationships are punctuated by weekends and brief vacations eagerly awaited and commonly discussed in language that boils down to "What a relief!" What is relieved is more than the particular tensions created by a difficult or unpleasant classroom episode. It is the unceasing experience of being surrounded by people whose constant gaze and responses are the permanent environment of every classroom.

The crucial consequence of the lengthy and sustained nature of classroom relationships is that people have many opportunities to influence those around them. Their continued exposure to one another provides endless occasions for each to be helped or harmed—enough occasions of vulnerability and dependency to overwhelm any strategy for self-protection. No matter how carefully teachers maintain their decorum, and no matter how carefully students use compliance and conformity to avoid attracting unwanted attention, the sustained long haul of classroom life makes everyone vulnerable to well-chosen jibes and well-timed refusals to cooperate. There is no escaping the fact that the same people will be in class tomorrow, next week, next month, and must be dealt with then. This sustained, enforced relationship among classmates and teachers forces them to learn to deal with each other, in ways that may either promote or undermine serious teaching and learning.

The Shared Properties of Classrooms

These characteristics of classroom life are so ordinary as to appear obvious; their significance is that they are consistent, unifying themes of classroom life, and can no more be taken from classrooms than stars can be taken from the sky. What is important is that the experience of being surrounded and vulnerable is part of life in *all* schools: in cities and suburbs and small towns, in advanced placement and remedial tracks, in kindergarten and high school. The shared experience of vulnerability means that all classrooms, effective and ineffective alike, have a great deal in common. This vulnerability is not part of other settings in which people are likely to find themselves on a daily basis, such as factories, offices, restaurants, shops, and neighborhoods. Instead, classrooms resemble more extreme settings—combat platoons whose members depend on each other for life itself, and close marriages and families, with their intense, continual vulnerability.

In classrooms, intense interactions, mutual scrutiny, long-term dependency, and the vulnerability they produce are part of everyone's daily life, and form a core relationship among people that shapes the ways in which they work together. Their shared vulnerability is not necessarily unpleasant, but is a constant reminder of how surrounded they are, and how much they depend on the people around them. Teachers depend on receiving the attention and clear responses of their students; they can't teach without these things, and students know it. Students depend on their teacher and classmates for cues about assignments and about what behavior will be valued and what punished. For both teachers and students, their vulnerability forces them to turn to one another for the agreements, assistance, and consent that they need to get what they want in the classroom.

The extraordinary similarity among classrooms has escaped attention because of our eagerness to sort them into good and bad. Imagine what different ideas would have occurred to biologists had they ignored the basic similarities among mammals, or bacteria; they would have been unable to understand fundamental life processes, and therefore unable to build the systematic knowledge that is the basis of modern biology and medicine. The core relationship of shared vulnerability in classrooms has an importance and range of implications comparable to that of the shared properties of each species, whose identification has led to many of the key advances in biology.

Classroom vulnerability is an unshakeable constant—a fact of life that does not depend on subtle variations of school or classroom organization—and it has powerful consequences for every education policy and every effort to reform the schools. These consequences begin with the effect of vulnerability on the nature of power in classrooms, a subject to which I turn in the next chapter.

CHAPTER 3

Power over Everyone Else:
Interactions That Control Classrooms

Most people think of power in the classroom as something that belongs to the teacher. The conventional view is that teachers are supposed to be in control of what happens in their classrooms; if they are not, then something is wrong. There are two problems with this view of power in classrooms: it is a wildly inaccurate description of how classrooms work, and it misconstrues the role of power in classrooms—its use by both students and teachers to shape teaching and learning. Power is the ability to shape events to one's liking, an ability possessed by every person in the classroom. They use it to get what they want and to undermine and alter official school policies that have been imposed on classrooms.

Teachers depend on their students to do the work of learning, a situation that creates endless opportunities for students to influence the teacher, rewrite classroom rules, and generally to place their own concerns at the center of life in their classroom. When teachers describe life in classrooms, they talk about the energy and ideas that students bring to school and impose on everyone around them. (Even passive students impose their influence on others by refusing to participate in activities that they reject.) My interviews with teachers found these characterizations of students' power, in classrooms ranging from kindergarten to high school:*

You're only the authority figure if they think you are. Not because you think you are. They have got to buy into that. And they're going to respect you a lot more if they think that you're caring, if they think that you're intelligent, you know what you're talking about, and you have a real honest-to-goodness concern about their welfare and their well-being. Because obviously they could say, "This means nothing to me." Well, it may not. And I would say to them, "I understand. It may mean nothing to you right now, *but.*"

As a teacher, you can't just go in with your own agenda and ignore what's going on with them. Because it doesn't work. Because if you did that Monday, you'd still see them Tuesday, but Tuesday they'd be a little bit angrier at you, and they'd be a little bit more resistant to what you're doing, and by the time you hit Friday it would be a disaster. I guess it's good, in that it forces you as a teacher to be more responsive to the students, and it forces *them* to be responsive, too.

They make the rules. They have made all the rules in the room. Anything that happens in the room, it's them.

When you're saying something and kids are just kind of looking at you and blinking and going "Huh," you know that

*The quotations in this chapter come from teachers who describe their own role in classroom interactions and the role of their students. While it is likely that students would describe the same interactions somewhat differently, I have chosen to use only teachers' reports to maintain a consistent point of view.

you're not answering their questions. They're not going to say, "No, that's not really what I mean," they just go "Huh, What are you talking about," and that's it, that's what you get from them. But at least then I know; and I've gotten a little bit better about finding out from them what the real question is.

One of the remarkable characteristics of these reports is the teachers' depiction of the give-and-take between themselves and students. Clearly, they know that their students have power. Similarly, students know that teachers have power: they make decisions about grades, they can send students to the principal's office, and they are bigger, older, and more knowledgeable. Despite these apparent disadvantages, students strive to influence their classmates and their teachers; at the same time, teachers are working to influence their students.

When a teacher gives students an assignment, the students may decide to cooperate—or they may decide to resist, by complaining or suggesting a modification in the teacher's plan. The teacher then has a choice: to insist on the original assignment, or to modify it. Both responses have prices attached to them. Insisting on the original assignment requires monitoring students closely, explaining precisely what students are to do, and enforcing compliance on resistant students; modifying the assignment means giving up the planned lesson in favor of a revised one, while still having to monitor and enforce compliance to a modest extent. In both cases, the students have shaped the experience of carrying out the assignment as much as the teacher has. Both share the ability to control teaching and learning in the classroom; that is, they share the power to determine their classroom's success or failure.

Shared Vulnerability Creates Power

Paradoxically, it is vulnerability that creates opportunities for teachers and students to control the people and events in their classrooms: the same vulnerability that places them at the mercy of the people who surround them makes everyone equally vulnerable and susceptible to influence. Thus, the crucial result of classroom vulnerability is that it creates the conditions necessary for the use of power.

As the previous chapter showed, each person in a classroom is able to affect how the others are treated, which means that teachers and students can choose strategic moments to influence their classmates. Power also is created by their mutual scrutiny. When everyone in the classroom is being scrutinized by everyone else, they acquire detailed knowledge that can be used to decide precisely how and when to influence those around them. Finally, classroom power arises from the fact that teachers and students know their relationship will be lengthy and sustained; they know that they will have plenty of time and opportunity to influence classroom events. Thus, the basic features of classroom vulnerability are also the raw materials of power. Because everyone in the classroom is vulnerable, everyone also possesses a measure of power.*

---

*The definition of power that has emerged from a great deal of analysis by political scientists is this: a person has power when he or she is able to shape events by exerting or making known his or her preferences. In other words, power is "causation by preferences," rather than causation by money, force, or persuasion, a definition laid out in 1975 by the political scientist Jack H. Nagel in his book *The Descriptive Analysis of Power*. Causation by preferences covers the whole range of events that involve power, and it certainly applies in classrooms. Nagel also offers an explanation for the failure of school people and education policy analysts to notice the forms of power that exist in classroom life. He observes that people who are sympathetic to a system, or who are part of that system, tend not to see it as involving power, which explains the fact that few people involved with education associate power with students and teachers.[1]

Consider, for example, the situation of students who need assistance because they do not understand an assignment, and teachers who need students' attention when they introduce a new lesson. Even though the students need the teacher's help, they can decide *when* and *how* to ask for it, and can then decide whether to comply with the assistance that is given. The students have already seen what happens to classmates who request help, and can use this knowledge of the teacher and of past classroom events to their advantage: they can signal, "Please help me, but on my terms; and if things go badly for me, I will withdraw, or become silent, or ask a stream of questions, or even disrupt the class."[2] In other words, by taking account of past events students can ask for help in ways that are likely to affect the teacher's response (by asking for an explanation or a demonstration, or by subtly threatening to disrupt the class). They clearly are dependent on the teacher, but can make it clear that the teacher depends on their cooperation as well. The students are both vulnerable and powerful, and can choose actions that take advantage of this.

Teachers who need the class's attention are also vulnerable and powerful. They can call out the names of the noisiest students, signaling the possibility of unpleasant consequences. They can simply try to present the lesson itself in an interesting way. Or they can use the heavy artillery of discipline and verbal harassment. But because teachers know that they must get along with their students for the rest of the year, often they will refrain from humiliating or strongly criticizing a student, and avoid actions that are likely to provoke disruptions. When a teacher is asked by a student for help, he or she may hesitate before responding, answer the student's question with another question, point out someone who has managed to solve the problem, or encourage the student to keep trying.[3] If a teacher responds to every request for help by immediately showing that person exactly what to do, the effect is to show the rest of the students in the classroom that they can ask for help instead of working it out for themselves.

When a student requests help, and when a teacher tries to get the class to pay attention, both are highly vulnerable. Their response is to try to control the people to whom they are vulnerable. Both can influence those on whom they depend; thus both have power, and both are subject to the influences imposed by their partners in the complicated mixture of vulnerability and influence that controls teaching and learning.

Reciprocal Power

In the classroom crucible, teachers and students always have power over the people around them. Students who need help can implicitly threaten to disrupt the classroom if they are treated badly; teachers can threaten equally dire consequences if students don't pay attention. There are, in fact, endless ways for teachers and students to use their power to influence each other, as these teachers report:

> They really have a lot of power, even when we pretend that they don't. I had a student teacher—kids really picked it up that she wasn't fond of them, they used to call her Miss Whatchamacallit. "Oh, what is your name again?" She'd been here for eight weeks. They're treating her the way she treats them, in their own little kid way. They're letting her know that we don't respect you because you don't respect us. Kids at any age can do things like that. I know they didn't think to them-

selves, "Yeah, we'll call her Miss Whatchamacallit and that will really piss her off, because we don't like her." But I'm sure they felt like, why even bother to learn your name when you don't even bother to say hi to us when we walk in in the morning?

Sometimes when they are fighting me, I have to spend time in *endless* explanations. I have a *large* number of kids saying, "I don't understand"—some of it, obviously, just thrown up as *barriers*. They say, I can't do it, I'm not going to try to do it, she asked me to do something that's impossible. And it [teaching and learning] would stop right there, when they do that.

The kids do put you through a training program; they will ask, do you know this, and will check you out on it. The other day in the honors sophomore class, I said that you're going to have to know the presidents, in order; you're going to be asked questions that relate to it. And one kid said, I bet you don't know it. I said okay, I'll go through it with you. This is just straight authority challenge and you have to respond. If you don't know it, you have to admit that you don't, but say you'll learn it. If you do know it, you're going to have to show them. And he said, wait a minute, flipped open the back of the book to the list, and I recited them. And he said, God, you *do* know it. And I said, and you're going to, too. You can't get angry with them for doing it; they'll call you on stuff like this, all the time. Even in the best of kids, there's always a certain amount of hostility.

An individual incident that sticks in my head is being threatened with a rock by a very large boy. I really thought he was going to hit me with it. And all I could do was sort of one of these Gunfight at the OK Corral things; stalk down the aisle, "Give me that rock, Richard." He did. I had no confidence that he was going to.

> When Greg was really frustrated, if I corrected him or I
> told him he had to go out on the cool-off chair to take time
> out to think about it—he'd say, You dummy! And the [other]
> kids would go, You can't talk to Elizabeth like that!

In the remarkable and fascinating form of power that exists
in classrooms, everyone has power, and each person is subject
to it; that is, every person in the classroom is partly controlled
by the people he or she aims to control. The most appropriate
name for this phenomenon is *reciprocal power.*

Reciprocal power exists in a group when each member
achieves a degree of control over the others and is simultaneously subject to control by them. It follows that every use
of reciprocal power combines an attempt to influence others
with an awareness of the power that others hold. The student
who slows down the class by saying that she doesn't understand knows that she must then listen to another explanation
of the assignment. The teacher who confronts one misbe-
having student is thinking about how the others will respond
to the scene. In classrooms, no controller can escape knowing
that he or she also is being controlled.*

By its very nature, reciprocal power is never concentrated
in a single person; it is highly dispersed among the people
in a classroom. They can decide to argue or cooperate, to
offer help or withhold it, to work with others or disrupt
others' work. These actions are powerful determinants of

---

*Nagel discusses what he calls the "symmetric view of causality," which is his
term for reciprocal power, arguing that "symmetric" power relations are rare in
politics and government; however, he is, in his words, "forced to admit" that such
cases of "interacting preferences" reciprocally related to each other do exist.[4] Another distinguished scholar, Richard E. Neustadt, wrote that "as between a President
and his 'subordinates,' no less than others on whom he depends, real power is
reciprocal and varies markedly with organization, subject matter, personality, and
situation." The power of the Presidency, he writes, is only "the power to persuade"—
not to command.[5]

classroom events, and they shape the ways that each classroom works.

The dispersal of power in classrooms means that control is spread and shared among the people in each classroom; all have the capacity to shape the lesson. Students and teachers negotiate about what the classroom's work will be:

You get the negotiations concerning what happens if they start talking to one of their friends, how are you going to respond to that; are you going to allow that to happen, ignore it if it's quiet, embarrass them so that they don't do it again? They're trying to figure out what kinds of actions work. And then on my part, I'm also trying to figure out what I can ask of them. For example, the first Friday I give homework, if I get a huge protest, then I'm all of a sudden thinking, is this worth it? [Laughs.] I found with one group that I ended up giving—having to give—the Friday assignment on Thursday so they could do it ahead of time, and that was the way we worked it out. So I felt that I was able to give a Friday assignment and they felt that they were getting away with not having a weekend assignment.

[In a kindergarten class] They affect me with their actions: all of a sudden they walk across the room, they get up, they twist around, they do something to another student—ignoring me, being slow to sit down, being noisy. They use their bodies to say what they want. All of them are totally capable of grabbing my attention when they want to.

If a kid is an influential type of kid, he can get all these other kids on his side, and they can all begin that stuff. And then you have a major behavior problem in the classroom. They can play off one another in a negative way. And it becomes a power struggle.

When you have a class that works, there's an incredible amount of energy there. There's so much energy that for the next week, you feel great. That energy doesn't come from me, it comes from them. Maybe it [instruction] works because they've gotten us, the teachers, to play their game. [Laughs.]

In the classrooms these teachers describe, every student is capable of influencing classroom events.

Another source of the dispersal of reciprocal power throughout the classroom is lengthy and enforced contact. Since the same classroom members must continue to deal with each other for the whole school year, the resolution of disagreements and conflicts is often only temporary; a student or teacher who is dissatisfied can always reopen the issue at a time and place that promises a different outcome. By contrast, reciprocal power cannot exist in short-term relationships, or in relationships that people can break off whenever they choose. In lengthy, sustained relationships, every negotiation is affected by the relationship's history, and by expectations and desires for the future. For example:

I had a problem about letting two of the kids go on a field trip; and I finally did let them go. This is what I thought: what is this going to do to my relationship to this kid *for the rest of the year?* And I thought, it's not worth it. I will never get anything out of her for the rest of the year, she will always remember this. That's an example of where I could have really screwed up a relationship, because I was ticked off; I would never have gotten this kid on my side if I had done that.

People in classrooms depend on each other for more than the terms of the deal at hand—they depend on each other for their quality of life for the rest of the year. In classrooms, disputes are never really finished; a teacher's short-term victory at the expense of a student can easily be only the first round in a continuing conflict.

At the same time, the classroom's sustained contact means that teachers and students have endless opportunities to respond to their classmates' resourcefulness and power with power of their own. For example, a teacher trying to stop a fight between students will call out their names; the end of their anonymity guarantees that there will be a price to be paid later on, in the next round of school life. Students, too, have many chances for comebacks. In classrooms, every action invites an equally powerful rejoinder; the threat of those rejoinders creates reciprocal power.

> I knew I was going to have that child in my room for the rest of the year, and it was only February. And my aim was to make things so that that little boy would be happy and could work for the rest of the year.

> When they are being sullen and refusing to talk—oh, how I hate that one. They can really get you with that. So I try to cozy them out of it.

These teachers know that success depends on their students' consent and cooperation—which gives students a great deal of power in the classroom.

Adjusting to Other People's Preferences

The constant mutual scrutiny that students and teachers are subjected to creates reciprocal power in two ways: it makes students and teachers aware of how much other people in their classroom affect them; and it simultaneously shows them how they can best influence those around them.[6] Because they receive constant reminders of how much the quality of their daily lives depends on other people in their classroom, teachers and students quickly learn to protect themselves by taking account of their classmates' preferences. They adjust their actions, and then gradually adjust their desires and preferences, in response to the realities of what they are able to obtain from people in their classroom: the kinds of help, support, friendship, and cooperation there, as well as the hostility, withdrawal, and refusals to cooperate. This happens slowly, as members of a classroom get to know each other. As the school year unfolds, classroom members acquire increasingly solid evidence about what they can expect from each other: how they will be treated, how other people will respond to their demands, and what kinds of help or hassles they are likely to get. Everything teachers and students know about their classmates slowly becomes an integral part of their preferences regarding the daily work of teaching and learning.*

They watch each other—that's really a biggie in kindergarten. The ones that don't know how to act, they sort of pretend that they do, and pretty soon they do.

You're out on a limb; working with a group of kids is always being in front of a crowd. You felt they were judging you, even if they weren't. But we feed off each other, too. You have to work hard to make it work; it's like being married, kind of.

---

*John Goodlad, the distinguished author of *A Place Called School*, reported that over 75 percent of the teachers in his extensive sample said they were "greatly influenced in what they taught by two sources—their own background, interests, and experiences; and students' interests and experiences."[7]

These teachers are describing how mutual scrutiny creates reciprocal power: the kids watch each other and draw each other out; and the teachers watch the kids, who watch their teacher and their classmates. Everyone in the classroom adjusts their behavior to mesh with that of the people they see around them.

The process of taking into account other people's preferences is a crucial aspect of reciprocal power.

> If I'm doing a lesson and I see that they just can't sit another second, I say, Okay, I'm tired of this, how about you, and they'll go, Yes, and I'll say, But we have to come back to this later, and they'll say, okay. And usually when we come back to it, then you'll have their attention.

This teacher has changed her actions and preferences in response to her students; they have agreed to do the same for her. Each use of reciprocal power reflects the preferences of the person who is acting, and also contains aspects of other people's preferences. In classrooms, everyone's preferences matter and all are powerful.

Teachers and students change their preferences in two ways: through feedback and through anticipation.[8] Feedback works by showing a person that his or her actions are ineffective, will not achieve the desired goals, and therefore must be changed. When a teacher tries a new way of presenting a lesson, the students' reactions make it clear within minutes whether or not the lesson is working. This feedback from students alters the teacher's thinking and actions, and creates new preferences that guide that teacher's actions in the future.

> You just start taking clues from the kids. It's amazing, the things that come out. It comes from really watching the group

intensely. Things like, Are they listening, paying attention, who in the group is not connecting?

In the first week, I got to find out what they could do and what they wouldn't do and what they wanted to be pushed to do, and that was great.

The kinds of feedback I'm looking for from them—are they interested or are they looking at the clock every five minutes? When I first began teaching I did a lot of the kind of teaching most of us get in college, and it worked as far as keeping them from being . . . loud. [Laughs.] But the feedback I got was that they kept constantly looking at the clock, and at the end of the class they'd say, that took forever! Or they'd raise their hand and either ask to go to the bathroom constantly so they could get out of there, or even raise their hand and say, when do we get out of here? [Laughs.] Those are signs that the class is not working, when they ask you when are they getting out of here. If we're discussing something and they keep coming back at me with questions, then it means they're thinking about it and they're interested enough in it to want to know more than what they have to know for the quiz.

I find if other teachers come up to me and say, Oh, you wouldn't believe it but one of the huge lunchroom conversations today was about Adolph Eichmann, then I say, *Okay!*—it must be working, because that's not part of their bargain with me—they don't have to talk about it outside the classroom, but if they do that on their own then I know something's working. I do adjust the way I teach a lot depending on what's working and what's not working. If I find they respond really well to doing independent work, and enjoy that, then I'll increase that.

They'll tell me if they're not listening—they'll say, this doesn't make any sense to me. Or they'll walk out of the classroom. Or they'll act out in some way. I find out if I'm effective if kids' heads start going down; then they're not listening.

These examples of feedback point out how frequently a teacher's approach is changed by students' reactions to a lesson.

People in classrooms also change their actions and their preferences in anticipation of their classmates' demands— they choose their actions with other people's wishes in mind.[9] For example, when students want to be accepted by their friends, they alter their preferences in anticipation of those of their friends: they like the same clothes and the same TV shows. When students want to be rewarded by their teacher, they incorporate that teacher's preferences into their own. Likewise, a teacher trying to gain the trust of a withdrawn student will try to anticipate that student's preferences.

For me, because I like to be positive, and I don't like to be negative and mean and punishing—my nature is to smile and like everybody and want them to be happy in the first grade— I will say something like, If you're having a hard time sitting still right now, you can get up and sit at a table. Some children might do that; and some children need to be named—I need to say, Emily, it's hard for you right now; why don't you go sit at a table.

For instance, it can be that you've planned an activity for the last half hour in the afternoon. And because of how much work they did in the morning, or how much sugar they had for lunch, or whether they got to play outside or not—you just might get to that time of the day when you realize that you can't do that. Nobody will get anything out of it. And you'll have to spend too much time keeping people quiet. They need to do something else. So you have to be able to change in midstream, and just—do something else.

Teachers and students anticipate each other's preferences in order to control each other.

Undermining Domination

Classrooms also provide their members with the power to withhold their support, and to subvert other people's demands. Reciprocal power enables teachers and students to undermine any attempt at domination by a single person in the classroom. When someone attempts to dominate classroom events—a student disrupts the class, or a teacher assigns homework that students regard as pointless—the first thing that happens is that people on the receiving end notice the methods that have made it possible. Mutual scrutiny and the intimate size of the classroom allow teachers and students to see precisely how they are being pressured: by a student's curses, or a teacher's grading policy, for example. They can also figure out the times and situations when it will be difficult to continue dominating them: when everyone ignores the disruptive student, or when students withhold their participation from a class discussion. They see what the controller's special sensitivities are: sarcastic putdowns, indifference, rejection. By watching and waiting, they learn to choose the time and place best suited to turning the tables on their tormentor. All of this knowledge has the effect of shifting control back to the people who have been controlled; first they see how to evade, then how to respond, and finally how and when to counter any attempt at one-sided power. In reciprocal power, control oscillates back and forth between any dominant person in the classroom and the others.

Reciprocal power is therefore very different from the authoritative, commanding power of presidents, generals, and corporate chiefs. These familiar culture heroes are actually exemplars of a single variety of power: domination of the many by the few, through the authoritative decisions of a hierarchy—a government, army, or corporation. In this form of power, one person is commander and the other people are commanded. Many people think that teachers have the power to dominate students, but their vulnerability makes this impossible. Even the most assertive teachers are subject to students' reciprocal power, because they need students to comply with their demands. The shared nature of classroom reciprocal power is reflected by these teachers:

> But the students are running the show; you just try to not let them know that! [Laughs.] But they know it too. It's a really odd arrangement.

> There's usually one or two kids in every single class who are just, in charge. And what you do is you allow them to be in charge—Okay, you are my co-teacher on this, help me out, what do you think, do you think a five-page paper is too long, do you think a three-and-a-half page paper would be better? You do a lot of negotiating.

> I once had a student who would walk out of the classroom; and what that does is it takes away my power in the classroom, and the other students are affected by that. So I said to him, If you have to walk out of the classroom, that's fine, but you have to tell me, "I can't take this, I have to leave." That step, for that student, not only helped that student out, helping him to recognize what his difficulty was, but it helped me out

too, because the other students were aware of the fact that he was at least recognizing my position in the classroom enough to tell me what was going down. You cut your losses in some situations.

Reciprocal power blurs the sharp separation between the powerful and the powerless. In reciprocal power, one person's strength does not guarantee that he or she will prevail, because the preferences of the (seemingly) strongest slowly come to embody certain aspects of the preferences of the (seemingly) weak.[10]

Teachers and students tend not to think of themselves as being powerful, despite their constant use of reciprocal power. As Seymour Sarason points out, ". . . at all levels (teacher, principal, administrator) there is the feeling of individual impotence."[11] To school people, classroom life often feels like an unending struggle, with the odds stacked against success; the main sensation of life in the classroom crucible can be one of being at other people's mercy. Instead of making them feel powerful, reciprocal power draws teachers' and students' attention to the power of the *other* people in their classroom. They become intensely aware of their dependence on those with whom they share the classroom. Students need opportunities for success and recognition, and these rewards are controlled by their teachers and classmates. Teachers need the attention and compliance that can only be provided by their students. Each use of power reminds everyone in a classroom how vulnerable they are to the people around them, and it simultaneously blinds them to their own modest ability to control events.

The fact that teachers and students do not see themselves as powerful controllers of classroom events does not diminish the impact of their power. Reciprocal power may be hidden from teachers and students by their vivid experiences of vulnerability, but its effects are just as significant as those of any other form of power. Reciprocal power changes their behavior, their preferences and the ways that they think; the result is that it transforms the work that is done in classrooms.

Control of Teaching and Learning

Teachers and students use their reciprocal power to impose a multitude of adjustments on teaching and learning in their classrooms, adjustments which have the effect of drastically reshaping each classroom's methods of instruction over the course of a school year.

- Reciprocal power affects classroom presentation methods, use of textbooks, and the willingness of students and teachers to participate in discussions.
- Reciprocal power speeds up or slows down the classroom's pace of instruction.
- Students use reciprocal power to make major and minor adjustments in their teacher's behavior and that of their classmates, sometimes making certain forms of instruction possible or impossible.
- Teachers use reciprocal power to alter the ways students approach their lessons.
- Reciprocal power shapes present and future assignments. The give and take between a teacher who explains an assignment and students who respond by asking questions and requesting help revises that assignment and molds everyone's expectations about future assignments in that classroom.

Every time reciprocal power is used, the classroom's methods of teaching and learning are subtly shaped.

The other day, when I was team teaching, I gave them a reading to do by the next day, and Ann [the other teacher] said, Why do you want them to read it by tomorrow, it's forty pages, they're not going to read it by tomorrow. And I said, Forty pages, they can read forty pages by tomorrow. And she said, That's right—they can read forty pages by tomorrow, but they won't, and then your lesson will be dead. Of course the next day half of them had read half of it, and they felt lousy, and I felt lousy and was angry at myself.

In some cases there are things that are not worth the hassle; and you have to be able to identify which is which. [Laughs.] You know, is this worth it? Or is it not worth it?

There can be a series of badgering questions, idiot questions, time-consuming questions, nit-picking questions, which can go on all year. I can remember several classes that never worked right for just that reason. It doesn't take very many kids to do it; say five out of thirty.

In each of these examples, the teacher changed the planned instructional approach because of students' use of reciprocal power.

Reciprocal power can build up patterns of hostility and distrust, or confidence and comfortable competition, that affect the ways that teaching and learning are carried out. Students' energy and excitement can make an ordinary lesson work perfectly; their inattention and boredom can undermine a superb lesson. In classrooms where there is ongoing conflict, or where students are very withdrawn, it is difficult for teachers to use methods of instruction based on demonstrations, class participation, debates, performance, or science experiments. The bottom line is that the success or failure of any method of instruction depends on whether a classroom's members use their reciprocal power to support it, change it, or get rid of it entirely.

There's always the issue in school that it's *cool* to be indifferent, even hostile, to teaching and to what's going on in school. I've seen this happen even with academically motivated kids; a clutch of kids who evince sort of a constant hostility or indifference that will literally poison the rest of the class, so that they won't function in the way that they should—in any sort of classroom discussion, for example, you'll waste three-quarters of your time.

With the sixth period class, it's just that few; but they make the whole class hard for me. And I tend to not want to interact with them. Yesterday, I was going around to each of them, and I thought, why don't I do this more, I do it with the other classes. I was never really aware of that until yesterday. If I would work more with them, they would see that I'm not an ogre; and if they like me—this is so important, if the kids like you, they will do anything for you. Sad but true. Ultimately you have to let the kids know that you care about them.

I just had a class that was filled with kids that really put me to the grindstone. A huge amount of energy can go into dealing with kids who don't want to be there. Even if you have one in your class who really didn't want to be there, and was angry about being there, and wanted to take that anger out on you, it makes it really hard to teach the class.

Even classroom power struggles that are completely unrelated to instruction can lead to major changes in teaching and learning; for example, when a student comes to class drunk, or angrily walks out of a class, the resulting struggle can change classroom relationships and lead to increased reliance on disengaged, unthreatening, rote instruction. Ordinary classroom life creates a stream of power struggles that is neither predictable nor controllable. It is the joint, unintended product of the people in each classroom.

Both teachers and students have the power to cast aside any approach to education they had previously accepted. Just as treaties among nations last only as long as they serve the interests of the signers, classroom agreements, too, are highly provisional. Teachers and students may fall into a routine, but it is wholly provisional. There are no unbreakable treaties; instead, there is a modest willingness to accept the existing working conditions until someone in the classroom pushes to overturn them.[12]

Reciprocal Power and Education Policies

Reciprocal power affects every school policy that attempts to regulate the actions of teachers and students. For example, if a policy requires daily homework assignments, the people in each classroom can use their reciprocal power to determine how the assignments will work. The people in some classrooms may make a tacit agreement that homework will be limited to brief reviews of work already done in class; in others, the classroom's members will accept different degrees of homework compliance from different students. When teachers and students use their reciprocal power to determine how homework will be done, the result is that they subvert the official schoolwide policy on homework. Classroom reciprocal power is so strong that it can reformulate every policy to suit the people in each classroom who must carry it out.

The way in which classroom time is used is particularly easy to alter. Teachers and students struggle over deadlines, the amount of time given to socializing and digressions, and the allocation of the scarce time available for students to demonstrate to the class what they have learned. Everyone can reallocate the classroom's time from work to distraction. The school's official policies that attempt to control the use of time in classrooms are subverted every day in every classroom.[13] Efforts to legislate the amount of time a classroom spends on instruction are inevitably futile.

Their behaviors force me to let them decide what my time and attention are focused on. On some level they know how their actions affect the class's time and attention.

They are very easily distracted if there's something going on next to them. If you're teaching a reading group, and you have something that you want to do, and somebody has another agenda—you have to take care of that first. You have to. Or you won't get anywhere. People outside of schools don't realize that—you can't expect that they're going to come through the door, and you'll have reading, and then you'll have math, and then you'll do this, and then you'll do that. Things happen, and you have to regroup, and reorganize, and shift gears, and do something else.

It can be *anything.* Sometimes a child will say, We read this *yesterday!* And then you have to either explain in *great* detail why you're reading it again, or why you *didn't* read it yesterday, you *thought* you did, you read something *like* it. You have to do that. [Laughs.]

Policies on classrooms' use of time are not the only ones undermined by reciprocal power. Official school policies on curriculum, textbooks, and assignments undergo a constant process of revision in classrooms.[14] The reading expert Jeanne Chall reports being told "many times" by teachers that in their classrooms, reading was not taught according to their school district's officially-endorsed reading program. Instead, they simply closed their classroom door, took their old phonics charts out of the closet, and taught in a way that suited them and their students. When Chall was taken to visit classrooms by school officials, the officials were often "quite embarrassed to find that the teachers were doing many things that were 'not permitted' " by school policy. What happened was that the teachers and students had used their reciprocal power to subvert the district reading policy in their classrooms.[15]

In the contest between official policies and a classroom's own approach to teaching and learning, the daily choices and adjustments of teachers and students steadily erode the official methods, turning them into something different, something of their own creation. In practice, this means that reciprocal power creates in each classroom a distinctive and personalized set of instructional techniques, methods of teaching and learning that are tailored to fit each classroom. Teachers' and students' on-the-spot inventions have the effect of redesigning teaching and learning in their classrooms.

One teacher summed up the way that daily classroom interactions control teaching and learning:

The give-and-take that goes on, things that I end up responding to, altering the lesson plan, changing what I do because of what a student does or something that happens among the students, or something that happens between me and a student that everybody is watching—that happens a lot. There might be a group that has enough children in it that lack appropriate self-control that might mean you really can't do what you had planned to do. And you might have a group that's much more low-key, and you can do different kinds of things with them.

This is reciprocal power at work. As later chapters will show, reciprocal power has utterly wrecked prevailing education policies.

CHAPTER 4

Why Classrooms Differ:
Classroom Membership
and Classroom Evolution

THE most consistent and dramatic finding of education policy research has been the discovery of classroom differences in student achievement. This chapter explains how classroom differences arise.

At the beginning of the school year, new classrooms are formed when groups of students are assigned to their new teachers. These new classroom members will share all of the experiences and events that take place there; the events in the classroom next door will be known only through observing from a distance or from gossip, and events that take place in other schools' classrooms are unlikely to be heard of at all. Their physical closeness to one another and their separation from other classrooms means that they can use reciprocal power to affect each other, while they remain essentially unable to reach beyond their classroom's walls to determine events in other classrooms. The fact that teachers and students are greatly affected by the actions of their own classroom's membership, but not by those of another, is the source of important differences between classrooms.

Classroom Membership and Reciprocal Power

Every classroom is composed of different people, who bring their own likes and dislikes with them. Their preferences dispose them to respond in particular ways to the activities and relationships that they encounter in their new environment. The members of a class also bring with them their own quirky behaviors and past experiences, to which other members respond. Teachers find themselves responding to "all these different variables" as they encounter each new class:

> [In the beginning of the school year] I have to be very careful about how I react to different children, because you don't know who is really supersensitive, and who you have to be a little more firm with. And it's not so much that a teacher before can tell you, either, because you're a different personality, and kids see you differently than they saw their other teacher.

> It's just simple logic: everybody is different. They've all come from different backgrounds and different pasts. [In first grade,] they've got five years of a past already. So everybody comes with their own little baggage. Even the teachers come with their own little baggage. You've got all these different little variables.

> It's very different—sometimes I have kids that just love to get into ideas, and take it to the nth degree; and sometimes I have kids that are very personally trusting, so that they really share very deep things about what's happening with them.

Some classes like very concrete activities; give them a sheet of paper and they feel more secure.

It's the mix of children, the personalities of the children and the teacher. This year my class is so different from last year. And it's the same racial balance and socioeconomic balance. Everything about it is the same, except I have a few more boys than girls this year. But this year the children are much calmer on the whole, I can talk to them like they're six-year-olds and get wonderful response from them; and last year I had children that were extremely sophisticated. The children demanded explanations for things, and it was just a totally different feeling in that classroom. It was a struggle.

"I don't like your attitude," a lot of kids say. "I don't like her clothes," or "She smells bad"—I mean, these are things I hear from kids, I'm quoting them. Or, "I just can't *stand* her personality, I can't stand it when she gets in my face." They come to you with this lifelong experience of all these things, and they may not like the subject, they may never have liked the subject, they may not like you, they may not like the room—they may not like the kids. There may be real significant things going on in their lives, beyond what goes on in school.

These highly personal preferences and attitudes form the basis of their responses to the other members of their classroom. If their classmates dislike them or their actions, they will find out quickly, through their classmates' use of reciprocal power. In contrast, they are unaffected by preferences of those in other classrooms, and by their patterns of reciprocal power.

With the passage of time, reciprocal power alters the classroom's relationships in response to the demands of the particular people within its walls. At the same time, the people in the classroom next door have their own preferences and responses and uses of reciprocal power that shape their classroom's unique relationships; thus, reciprocal power affects each classroom differently, building and intensifying the differences between classrooms.

The relationships that emerge in each classroom depend on who takes part in the process of reciprocal power there; because there are different people in each classroom, their behaviors and relationships gradually become different from those of other classrooms.

You can be teaching the same courses as last year, with kids who are very similar, and it's totally different. I have one class, my sixth period class, that's been giving me fits all year long. I realized that this is a highly creative bunch of kids, and I really do like them all, but because of these three or four kids who are like a little knot of kids, I have found myself lumping all of them together. You know, "I hate this class." It's the group dynamics working.

So I told the kids, It bothers me to do this, it seems like I'm always yelling at this class; but I really *like* this class. And one of the kids said, "Oh, yeah?" And she's one of the ones I'm talking about. But I look around at all these little faces, and most of the kids I do like, but the group dynamics in that particular class are such that . . . I struggle to try to maintain control. And in my first period class, almost twice the size, they're just nice, more jovial, more willing to listen. It's the kids and how they interact with one another, and with you, it doesn't matter how experienced you are. You can't control it.

Teachers will say that they had a really different experience this year than last year, and what they say is, this class just didn't want to learn. And they say, Oh, my freshman class, they're really great, my freshmen are just wonderful; that sophomore class, they're rotten. That's said by school people! And every class has a personality; every single class. Personal interactions, the interactions of those particular kids, make things happen that you've never seen before.

Every time you change the group of people in the class— every cycle [half semester]—everything is up for grabs. Every single time, it's completely different, just from the kids in the class. And it's very frustrating, because you figure out what's effective for one class, and you go into the next class saying "No problem!"—and you present this stuff and it absolutely flops. It's one of the worst feelings—because you don't know what to do then.

As reciprocal power causes people to adjust their own preferences in response to the other members of their classroom, the classroom becomes even more differentiated from its neighbors. Meanwhile, the people in neighboring classrooms have been adjusting their own preferences in response to those of their own classmates. Without ever intending to do so, teachers and students generally start behaving toward each other in ways that are distinctive to their own classroom. Classroom differences shape teaching and learning, too.

When I taught U.S. history last year I had two very different groups; both were the medium-ability groups in our school. I divided them into groups to do research on how the Depression affected different groups. In one class, the kids wanted to have a good report, so that when they gave their report to the class they'd look smart. In the other class, I tried the exact same lesson and it was chaos, and I spent the whole time running from one group to the next trying to make sure they weren't all talking about their boyfriends.

What this teacher is saying is that classrooms are ad hoc enterprises built by a particular group of people, out of their particular ways of interacting. Because classroom instructional methods are hammered out, patched together, then revised again throughout the life of each classroom, they simply are not transferable or exportable in the way that, for example, textbooks are.[1]

Students and teachers use reciprocal power to tailor their classroom's teaching and learning to fit them. Because of reciprocal power, the approach to teaching and learning that is used in a classroom is inseparable from the particular people who are members of that classroom.

> The weirdest thing about a classroom is that students are individual people learning in a very quirky, individual way, but they're also learning from this whole dynamic thing that's happening with the twenty-two other people in the classroom.

> After the first month and a half of school, you can see where it's going with them and what they want from you. You get twenty-seven very different little personalities. Some years it hasn't worked out. I really remember one year where we spent a whole year and they all absolutely hated each other. They never jelled. Never.

While a teacher may bring teaching methods from past classrooms, those methods will immediately be reshaped and revised by the students in the new classroom.

Does this mean, then, that a teacher gains nothing from years of experience in a variety of classrooms? To the contrary: experience helps teachers respond to the differences among classrooms. The value of a teacher's experience is not contained in a bagful of techniques that can be applied in the same way in every classroom, but in an understanding of the process of adjusting to each new group of students. Experienced teachers use that understanding as they carry out the work of discovering how to respond to the distinctive qualities of each new classroom. An experienced teacher knows that teaching and learning are irreducibly tied to the particular people who make up each classroom's membership.

An important lesson follows from this link between classroom membership and classroom behavior: change the membership of a classroom, and you will change the ways that teaching and learning take place there. Because students and teachers use reciprocal power in accordance with their own preferences and those of their classmates, adding to or subtracting from a classroom's roster inevitably changes how reciprocal power is used in that classroom. Changes in membership occur frequently in classrooms. When students are absent because of a long illness or truancy, their reciprocal power is subtracted from their classroom's relationships. In some classrooms, half of the students leave and are replaced by newcomers during the school year.[2] Student achievement suffers in such places, for those who stay as well as for those who leave. Richard Murnane's analysis of classroom achievement gains found a consistent pattern of reduced achievement in classrooms with high turnover, even after taking account of the prior achievement levels and socioeconomic status of the students he studied.[3]* When students leave their classroom, even if it is just for an hour of remedial reading assistance, they are not part of the relationships that are hammered out during their absence.[4] These changes in mem-

---

*This study, which uses the methods described in chapter 1 for measuring the effect of classrooms on student achievement, is one of the few efforts rigorously to examine the effect of turnover in a classroom's membership on the achievement of its students.

bership create changes in reciprocal power—and changes in teaching and learning.

The Evolution of Classrooms

Each classroom goes through a process of change that unfolds gradually over the course of the school year. Teachers and students share a history that begins in September and lasts until June—a long time, as is suggested by their sense of relief when June finally arrives. The long school year creates pressures on people in classrooms to get along with one another.

> It takes a long time to establish trust. You don't expect a student to walk in on Day One and think you're wonderful. Just don't expect it, don't be disappointed. That was a really tough lesson for me to learn, that there was not going to be immediate rapport.

> The testing and whatnot in the first term and a half of school tends to be much more concrete; it's confidence-building to a certain extent. It also gives the kids a fair read on what's going to be expected of me in this course and can I handle it.

> You spend the first two months making the contacts, trying out different things with the class, to see what will work or what won't. At the beginning of the year lessons are always shorter, because you want to try to see what works; so you try a variety of different techniques.

As these narratives show, the process of adjusting to a new classroom is an evolutionary one: there are pressures from the environment, trials of numerous possible solutions, and a kind of natural selection of solutions that are most closely adapted to each classroom's power relationships.

This classroom was absolutely wild at the beginning of the year. I have such an array of different personalities. At first, I didn't think I was going to make it through the year; I thought, please let me get sick. We spent so much time working out situations—acting out how it would be to not be able to hear, like the little deaf boy in the class. The kids started to have a whole new respect for this little boy, who was really in trouble, trouble, trouble. And now, since after Christmas, the whole room has changed. They're so accepting of him and he's finally accepting their friendship, and that they're not going to pull it out from underneath him, and he has settled in. A lot of stuff has happened from just who's in the room, in all different ways.

It's like a cycle—once you can get it to start working, then they feel good about the class, they do their work, so they do well, so you feel good about them. Last term, I got to the point where you say, What is the point of putting in extra effort for this class?—because they really don't care, and so you just come and do the minimum.

Whereas this term I've been doing extra research for them, to answer their questions, and I've been reading up on aspects of the Third Reich that I didn't know about before, and they're giving me feedback that they like the class, that it's interesting; they say thank-you to me at the end of the class each day! [Laughs.] It makes me go home and read more to try to make it even more of a success. There is a huge difference, even thought it's the same course and I'm the same teacher—it's just different kids, or kids who aren't that different but who for some reason do things differently.

These teachers are describing their classrooms' unpredictable evolution, from chaos to order and from failure to success. This evolution happens because the people in each classroom respond so intensely to how they are treated that they create a new classroom history.

The trigger that starts the evolutionary process is shared vulnerability. In the classroom, every mistake is noticed, laughed at—and remembered. When things go badly for teachers and students, they are put on the spot: their problems keep causing trouble and pain until they are resolved. For example, when a teacher's question is met with blank stares and incomprehension, the class comes to a standstill until the teacher figures out what to do. When a student is treated with contempt by classmates, the student's suffering lasts until he or she comes up with a way to change things. When people in the classroom crucible are subjected to these powerful, painful experiences, they begin to search for practical solutions to their problems—and the evolutionary process is triggered. A student or teacher who is on the receiving end of ill treatment needs to discover what will satisfy the other members of the classroom to make them stop behaving that way. The driving force that pushes teachers and students to search for ways of satisfying their classmates is, of course, the reciprocal power of the people who share their classroom. Reciprocal power is the pressure from the environment that powers the classroom's evolutionary process.

They come in, and there are a lot of strange children, and it's very scary. In this school, the first-grade teachers go and visit the kindergarten classes and talk to the children and let them ask questions about first grade. And even though we do that, it's still very scary for them. You don't realize just how scary it is even for children that seem to be afraid of nothing. It's—

it's what they don't know. I think it goes on in high school, too, in different ways.

Sometimes even as you're saying it, you feel foolish. Because you realize that person is thinking: she's talking about six-year-old kids! What could be the problem? How could it be difficult? And sometimes even the retelling of a story doesn't sound like anything happened; it minimizes it; and it might even sound funny, and people might laugh. At the time, of course, it wasn't funny at all. And you're at your wits' end trying to figure out how to cope with it, and what to do with it, right away. So I really haven't found a way to explain to nonschool people . . . I really try not to get into that aspect of my job.

If you're in first grade for about a week [as a teacher], *you learn the language.* You have to be extremely specific with them, because they interpret your words literally. You can't say, Here's your homework for tonight; *Night!,* they'll say; At *night!* I'm not gonna do it at *night!* So you can't say that. They're extremely literal. And they force you to be literal, too.

If somebody disrupts the class—you lose control of a student or a student walks out of the classroom—then you just fall into this deep lull and you have to jumpstart again. You have to find something that will get them.

Search

When teachers and students need solutions to their problems, they can look around their classrooms to see what other people have done in similar situations, and what happened in those situations. They search for solutions by looking for behaviors that have a history of being accepted by the other people in their classroom.[5]

> The kids in there have learned how to ask for help. Lots of kids would rather go down the drain than say, I don't get this. I've had kids go for algebra help, I've had kids go to their French teacher and say "I'm overwhelmed," and I think it's terrific. And they've watched each other—they say, Hey, Josh has gone for help; he's obviously a star student, and he feels good, so it must be okay for me.

Both teachers and students use precedents and the history of the classroom as a source of ideas for solving their problems—whether the problem is inattention, boredom, or poor attendance.

In order to be effective, the solutions that teachers come up with need to be tied closely to particular people and events in their own classrooms; for this reason, the classroom history serves as a better reference library of potential solutions than do events in other classrooms with other memberships. Previous classroom events provide teachers with clues to what might work this time, because they have already worked for this classroom: which students can safely be called on, how to avoid embarrassing a student, or how to make help available to lagging students without humiliating them. Depending on the classroom's history, a teacher might see the benefits of paying less attention to the classroom's star performers; or avoiding putting students on the spot with direct questions; or separating disruptive students by putting them on opposite sides of the room. These insights work because they have been seen to fit the people in a particular classroom:

> Sometimes the greatest things happen on the spur of the moment. That's why I hate those lesson plans. Because when

you're sitting at home, it's not your classroom. You realize that something is possible when you're right here in the middle of it. And it turns out *great*.

The pressures of the environment make students, too, look for proven ways to respond effectively to the other members of their classroom. If a student is ignored by the teacher or by classmates, the student can search for ways to recapture their time and energy by thinking about past responses to students who asked for help or who disrupted the class. The student has seen how other students get the teacher to spend time with them and what it is like between them; the times when it is allowable for students to talk while they work; and the demands for attention that are accepted, and those that are not.

As one teacher explained, "The students say, 'You can't do that' to each other based on what they've seen in the classroom before—it's like a precedent. Or they will accept something because it has been good for them before." Precedents are quickly noticed and adopted by students.

Selection and evolution

The ideas that result from classroom search are *relationship ideas*. They reflect an understanding of how people in a classroom can get along with each other,* and how they can cope with the work of teaching and learning. Each person in the classroom watches what the others do, and notices how well their strategies seem to work; at the same time, every ob-

---

*Howard Gardner argues in his book *Frames of Mind* that the ability to think clearly about human relationships and solve problems involving relationships is a critical ingredient in many kinds of learning and work.[6] Interpersonal intelligence appears to be involved in searches for ideas about how a particular group of classroom members can work together.

server is intensely aware of his or her relationship to those they are watching:

> They hear what other people have to say, and they see each other's work. Sometimes they cringe when people look at their work. It's not just what I say—sometimes they won't accept what I say—but they are cognizant of the other people in here, and what they're saying to the other kids.

The result of this self-awareness is that the watchers can tell that some classroom solutions aren't appropriate for them to imitate, while others can be copied immediately. To select the particular solutions they need, classroom members pay close attention to their roles in the group—their insiderness or outsiderness, and their support from classroom allies. Teachers and students adopt those solutions that mesh with their relationships in that classroom.

The link between classroom relationships and the search for solutions has an important result: it ties each classroom's ways of teaching and learning to relationships that have been adopted in that particular classroom. The development of relationships thus shapes the solutions used in each classroom, gradually increasing the differences between it and other classrooms. Howard Gardner explains why this connection is important:

> The interactions of human beings lie at the heart of the education process to a much greater extent than is true in manufacturing industries. Since relationships among human beings are by nature idiosyncratic . . . it is only a continual process of trial and error that produces effective techniques. A further source of complexity is the interdependence of motivations for particular behaviors on the part of students

and teachers in the same classroom. For example, the reaction of one student to a particular technique depends on the reactions of the other students in the class. Said differently, classroom atmosphere matters and is both volatile and difficult for a teacher to judge, much less control. Here too there is a continuing process of finding out what is working and what is not.[7]

Gardner's observations underline the fact that both teachers and students need the knowledge that can be found only by observing the other members of their classroom, their use of reciprocal power, and the results that follow. Their mutual scrutiny allows them to select ways of coping with classroom problems that have been successful.

In the critiques, they're a little bit careful if it's a classmate. Because they have to get along with them for the rest of the year. What's interesting is I always show them the other class. And boy—they'll go, "That stinks!" Even though they sometimes say negative things in critiques with their own class, I know that they're still holding back. And there's some value to that; there is a respect.

Thus, the precedents for behavior in each classroom set limits for its students and teacher. This selection process confirms an old description of human problem solving: people who have a problem consider as possible solutions ideas that are close at hand, rather than looking for solutions from outside their experience.[8]

In every classroom, people select behaviors that work for them and drop the ones that don't; the result is a process of evolution of teaching and learning, where particular instructional techniques are gradually adopted or dropped because of their past record in each individual classroom. Certain assignments may meet strong resistance from students, evolve into briefer assignments, or be replaced by other kinds of lessons. The teacher's choice of whom to call on will evolve to reflect their past performance and effect on the class. Homework assignments will gradually take into account the past behavior of students.

> With the seniors I had last semester, I found that the tools I usually use to negotiate with kids didn't work, and I was starting to have to flunk kids. That was the only thing that finally got their attention; I think they assumed that since they were seniors and they knew that if they failed my course they would have to go to summer school, that I wouldn't have the nerve to fail them. I ended up having to use tactics that I don't normally use, because we were coming from such different places on what our expectations for the class were. And then they treated me in ways that weren't normal for them, either.

Sometimes the search for successful classroom behaviors results in brilliantly effective ideas that greatly advance teaching and learning; sometimes it results in educational disasters: withdrawal from the work of the classroom, low expectations, and sustained failure. If teachers or students view classroom give-and-take as too risky to tolerate, they are likely to search for ways to minimize the amount of teaching and learning that takes place. Fear, withdrawal, and anger can exact a toll from classroom work.

With every problem that arises in the classroom, more searches are triggered and the catalogue of ideas grows. People discover ways of getting help and cooperation, ways of avoiding rejection and hostility, and ways of resolving conflicts and fights. They also discover what is not possible for them. If the catalogue of classroom events includes no examples of low-achieving students asking for and receiving help, then the idea that it can't and won't happen gradually gains force. Students then will search for ways to avoid participating in teaching and learning, and will discover a repertoire of acts of frustration and rebellion that can destroy a classroom's work.[9] Everything that happens in a classroom, good and bad, gets added to the catalogue of ideas that will be used by the members of that classroom in the future.

If you're the sort of person who likes to have every day planned out, you are going to find the differences in classes *very* disturbing, because some classes make it impossible to do that. For the rest of us, it's actually rather exhilarating. People who haven't done it assume, oh, you've written your lesson plans your first year, and then you do the same thing for the rest of your life. Even given the same lesson plan, in three different classes what you come out with is something entirely different in each case. Even the point that you end up making in the lesson will be different. How much of it you cover, what happens to become the focus, changes from one class to another.

The ideas that emerge from the classroom's evolution are not likely to reflect official school policies.[10] When students and teachers are busy figuring out for themselves how to cope with their classroom problems, obviously they are not following anyone else's game plan. Instead of fitting themselves neatly into the cookie-cutter shapes of official policies, teachers and students search for practical ideas that help them cope with the problems created by the other members of their classroom.* Teachers and students who discover that a

*This analysis of teacher and student problem solving can be interpreted as an argument against some kinds of teacher examinations (perhaps including some as-

particular method of instruction is painful for them cannot be convinced otherwise by official policies. The differences among classrooms are too great, their memberships too divergent, and the process of classroom evolution too deeply rooted to be overcome by policy statements and official pronouncements.

---

pects of the examinations being developed by the National Board for Professional Teaching Standards) that rely on hypothetical questions about what a teacher should do in a situation described in the exam question. If this chapter is correct, teachers' decisions depend directly on their knowledge of particular students in a particular classroom. The specific context of classroom relationships is inevitably absent from questions about "what to do if such and such a situation arises." A more useful type of examination might ask teachers to correct student essays, thus demonstrating teachers' knowledge of subject matter and their ability to identify students' mistakes.

CHAPTER 5

How Schools Influence Their Classrooms

THE education policy debate has unquestioningly asserted the importance of the school as an influence on students and teachers, despite the evidence that most of the variation in student achievement is within schools, rather than among them. Schools are said to be the key instruments of education policy (if so, they haven't done their job very well). Schools and principals are said to determine the "effectiveness" of their classrooms (an untested proposition, examined later in this chapter). What is missing from these theories about the alleged importance of schools is a clear picture of how and why teachers' and students' actions are *caused* by certain attributes of their school. This chapter shows how a school influences the actions of people in its classrooms.

The influence of schools on teachers and students has partly to do with their hiring of teachers, which clearly affects classrooms; partly with official school programs and policies, whose effects are often modest; and partly with a little-noticed but pervasive phenomenon: schools show teachers and students what their future holds, and teachers and students respond to what is shown to them. This phenomenon stems from the fact that most teachers and students know with considerable accuracy who will be in their classroom next year. An ordained and universally known sequence of school life is that students progress from one grade to the next every year, and teachers annually receive a new batch of students promoted from the previous grade. The sequence of grades, therefore, is also a sequence of classrooms. By taking note of the people who are likely to be members of their classrooms in the future, teachers and students can see how they will be treated and what experiences they are likely to have. Thus the school influences teaching and learning in its classrooms by showing teachers and students what the future holds for them.

The School Is a Sequence of Classrooms

While teachers and students cannot directly influence people in other classrooms in their school, they can observe them. This phenomenon turns the school into a message center: it conveys information to all of the people in the school, while leaving them to pursue their work in separate classrooms. Thus, schools link their classrooms without controlling them.

The message center works because teachers and students always know where they fit in their school's sequence of grades and classrooms. Tenth-grade teachers can tell by looking at ninth-grade classrooms who their students will be; the obvious things stand out: race, affluence, cooperativeness, truancy. Gradually, the more subtle qualities of students' lives can be seen, too: their interest in work, their willingness to trust, their desire to be in school or to be somewhere else.

We always know at the end of the year who will be in our classes; and we don't give that information to the parents, though, until school is ready to start.

Some kids want to please so badly; and some couldn't give a damn. [Laughs.] It's innate. In both cases. [Laughs.] Some of them couldn't give a damn if you're there or not, they're going to go off and do their thing and you can exhort them, you can chide them, you can be all over their case, you can cajole, you can threaten, you can promise, you can punish, and they're still going to revert to those silly-ass behaviors, the off-topic behaviors. And other ones are going to be so meek and mild that if you look at them cross-eyed they're going to cry.

These teachers are describing their knowledge about their next batch of students. As teachers observe other classrooms in their school, they get a clear picture of the students who will be in their future classes—a sort of consumer's guide to the personalities and events that will determine how a teacher is going to be treated in next year's classroom.

At the same time, tenth graders have their own consumer's guide when they look at the eleventh grade's classrooms. Most students can guess with considerable accuracy who their teachers are going to be the following year. They already know most of their future classmates. It is easy for tenth graders to judge what life is like for the eleventh graders; they are, after all, only a year older. It is easy to see whether their classes are energetic and engaging or empty and dull, through occasional glimpses into classrooms down the hall.

It's one of the few times in life that you've got a predictable future; you walk in there and you have, within certain limits, a predictable four years ahead of you. You can make plans for many things, whether it's that you're going to join the swim team, whether it's that you want to have Mr. Garhart for math in the eleventh grade, given that you do well in math and that sort of thing.

I'm a pretty tough teacher; kids know that; I don't get kids who have never heard of me. Everyone who comes into the room has their preconceived notions, which is true for any teacher, unless they are brand-new teachers and then they are known as brand-new teachers and they are fodder.

Kids say, Oh, this is the way Mrs. Hazelwood is, and this is what we do. We all have reputations, but that's true in any school. And I have the reputation that kids are afraid of me, and I like that. I've worked for that. And the way I know to do that is to give a lot of homework.

Teachers' reputations provide students with important information on how they can expect to be treated in the future. Many students also have older brothers and sisters in school, and the family grapevine tells them how they are likely to fare. Family connections provide information for teachers, too; they can guess from the actions of older brothers and sisters how their younger siblings may behave.

When people look around their school for evidence about how they will be treated in the future, what affects them most are images of how people like themselves are treated—what happens to, for instance, slow learners, or the teachers of slow learners, or students in the advanced track, or black students who come from the housing project, or middle-aged white teachers. They are less interested in how their classmates or teachers will be treated. Their perceptions of what their next classroom will hold for them are individual perceptions, and will vary even among people in the same grade and classroom.

One of the main differences [between students] is the level of anger and frustration. They sometimes come in with this huge amount of anger and frustration. And sense of failure. Generally I can coach them enough in that kind of situation that they won't fail, and they're happy with a D—if they get a D, some of these kids say Miss Chapman, I never ever passed history in my life before, and so that becomes a success. If you get a kid who is so frustrated and so sure of failure that she won't do anything for extra help, then that becomes . . . those are the kids that you end up feeling justified failing. It ends up being tough, because you look at them every day, and they're sitting there being angry, looking at their watch, needing coaching to do any activity or be called on.

A classroom often includes some students who expect to do well and others who expect to fail, based on their observation of the teacher and class in previous years.

One important consequence of the highly individual interpretations teachers and students make about their future prospects in school is that although the school provides them with maps of the future, the maps are different for each person. Some will see that people like themselves are treated well, and that their work will be rewarded with achievement and recognition; others get a map that shows few accomplishments or none, and a day-to-day life of sustained conflict, rejection, and discomfort. For many, the map contains mixed news: the likelihood of some good treatment and some less good; a few possible rewards and a number of problems.

Within any school, expectations for the future vary because

teachers and students know they will be assigned to different classrooms, and the differences matter. Students' expectations also may depend on their race. The federal government's school surveys show, for example, that blacks are more likely than whites to be placed in classes for retarded students, to receive corporal punishment, to be suspended from school, and are less likely to be assigned to classes for gifted students.[1] Consequently, black students have different expectations for the future than do white students. Teachers and students draw their conclusions about the future from the classrooms to which they are likely to be assigned in the future.

Because people act on the basis of what they expect from the future, their present classroom behavior tends to reflect their expectations about future classrooms.

> A really good school should have the image that tells even the kids who are not academically top of the line—that there are still a fair number of good possibilities for them, people who will be responsive to them, things that they can learn. That somebody is finally going to teach me to add fractions. That if there's a problem I have, there's somebody here who can address it. That even though I've got problems at this point, there *is* somebody here who can do something about it. Rather than, I'm going to have nothing but the no-goodniks in class, who are not going to do a damn thing, and it's not going to be possible for me to function and work. Either one of those expectations can be very important in somebody's life.

Teachers' and students' classroom behavior becomes involved or withdrawn, optimistic or pessimistic, contented or angry, depending on their expectations about their next classroom. If a teacher or student sees a future of working with people who would rather be somewhere else, who don't treat each other well, and whose energy and friendship are withheld, he or she will become discouraged and withdrawn. Hopeful visions of future classrooms can stimulate students and teachers, creating energy, persistence, and hard work. People's expectations for the future are the basis of their plans and choices in the present, so it seems apparent that people who expect to be treated well in future classrooms are unlikely to drop out, or (for teachers) to leave the teaching profession.

This view of the school—as a sequence of classrooms that enables teachers and students to see how they will be treated in the future and to respond to what they see—points to the perceptions and actions of teachers and students, rather than those of school officials, as the cause of the school's influence on classroom life. This argument again reminds us of the fact that education takes place in the classroom, and if a school policy is to influence education, it must be designed and operated so that it affects the behavior of teachers and students in classrooms. In general, policy makers are completely unaware of the power of the school's sequence of classrooms as a way to influence the behavior of teachers and students; the argument presented here attempts to remedy this failure.

Effective Schools Research

A fascinating contemporary example of the belief that schools, rather than classrooms, are responsible for student achievement gains has become known by the label of "effective schools research." The "effective schools" writers focused their attention on urban schools whose students scored above the average levels for poor and minority children. They argued that the success of these schools could be repeated elsewhere if other schools would follow a set of highly prescriptive policies found in many of the schools studied by these researchers. The new prescriptions quickly attracted publicity and gained political momentum.

The effective schools researchers—George Weber, Wilbur Brookover, Lawrence Lezotte, and others*—conducted studies of inner-city schools whose students scored above the average for their cities, and surveyed the principals at the schools. In these "effective schools," they found strong principals whom they called "instructional leaders" because they were actively involved in establishing policies for teaching and learning, rather than confining themselves strictly to administrative tasks. The researchers also found that in these schools, principals and teachers paid attention to test scores and kept track of how well each student was doing; that they shared a clear sense of mission, in the form of specific achievement goals for students; that safety and order prevailed in these schools; and that teachers held high and specific expectations for students' learning. According to the effective schools researchers, these school characteristics caused high student achievement among poor and minority children. Schools that adopted these characteristics would become effective, they argued. These ideas were extremely attractive to people searching for education policies that worked; there grew up around these and similar claims a self-proclaimed "effective schools movement" that promoted the policies.

Clearly, these schools were doing something right—but what was the root cause of their success? The problem with the effective schools research is that it assumes that prescrip-

*A summary of research and policy proposals associated with these writers, and a short bibliography, are presented in Lynn Olson, "Effective Schools."[2] This summary is particularly useful because little of the quantitative empirical research on which the effective schools movement is based has been published in the major, refereed scholarly journals.

tive policies, rather than principals' and teachers' adaptations to their students, are responsible for high achievement. The researchers did not identify those policies that preceded the schools' records of high achievement; instead, they identified the policies that were in use *after* the researchers discovered the schools' successes. That is, the policies may have been the result of teachers' and principals' successes, rather than their cause. A school's policies are often the consequence of a long history of classroom events in that school; a policy often gets adopted by school officials to ratify a pattern of classroom teaching and learning that has evolved over time. This possibility was not considered by the effective schools researchers, because they were searching for policies that could easily be transplanted to other schools.

There are two plausible explanations for the shared policies that were found in high-achieving inner-city schools. First, there simply may have been a history of high student achievement (due to the work of teachers and students) that prompted officials in these schools to adopt these policies. High test scores can easily cause principals and teachers to have high expectations for the future, to take on a sense of mission and an academic orientation, and to pay increased attention to students' test scores. A history of achievement encourages officials to take credit for their classrooms' accomplishments and to try to sustain them. Thus, the effective schools' policies may have been adopted as the result of high student achievement that had other causes.

The second likely explanation for the effective schools policies is that they were side-effects of *classroom* events that were the real cause of the students' high achievement. For example, high student achievement may have been caused by the gradual growth of an experienced and skilled teaching staff in a given school; simultaneously, the teachers' increased knowledge and experience could have led them to take actions that fostered a climate of safety and order. The school's safety and order would thus have been a by-product of teachers' increased skill in dealing with classroom problems. In the same way, skilled teachers could be the real source of the principal's role as an instructional leader, by reducing student disciplinary problems and thus giving the principal the free time to become involved in instructional issues. Again, the principal's involvement in instruction would have come about *after* teachers and students improved their behavior. All of the policies that researchers have found in the effective schools studies seem more likely to be by-products of successful education than the cause of it. Successful classrooms may have created the appearance of effective school policies that never existed.

With so much attention focused on policies thought to be capable of creating effective schools, something important has been lost. The impressive accomplishments of some students and teachers in inner-city schools has been almost forgotten. The significance of these schools is the proof they provide that giving up on such schools and the children they serve is a wholly unnecessary waste of human lives. By downplaying the accomplishments of teachers and students, and concentrating their research wholly on policies and management, the effective schools writers may have mistaken the container for the contained. Schools are, after all, containers for the work that is done every day by teachers and students.

Can prescriptive policies turn ineffective schools into effective ones? So far, there has not been a carefully monitored experiment that would identify a group of low-achieving schools, and then systematically introduce the effective schools policies to see if they lead to changes in student achievement.* In the absence of such an experiment, there is little empirical support for the claim that school policies (rather than a complicated mixture of history, teacher recruitment, and hard work in classrooms) actually are responsible for the achievement record of the schools studied by the effective schools writers. The schools that have tried their approach have tended to modify their prescriptions, according to journalists' reports;[3] not surprisingly, the effective schools movement has run into the same ineluctable differences between classrooms that confront all prescriptive education policies.

Changing Classrooms by Changing Schools

The great diversity of messages students and teachers get from their school concerning their futures means that most schools are not the strongly centralizing, assimilating force that officials and policy makers imagine them to be. Classroom reciprocal power and the classroom differences it creates are evidence of the *decentralizing* nature of schools. It is individual classrooms shaped by teachers' and students' reciprocal power that control teaching and learning; centralized school policies in most schools are just talk. The idea of the school as a unifying force is based on the assumption that standardized policies and curricula cause people to behave

*To be credible, the experiment should identify a group of low-achieving schools, randomly assign them into an experimental group or a control group, and then introduce the effective schools policies into the experimental group of schools (but not the control group). Comparing student achievement in the experimental and control groups would then provide a valid measure of the impact of the effective schools policies.

in standard ways—that rules cause people to conform to the rules. Current education policy is based on this assumption. However, the diversity of students' and teachers' responses to their school means that schoolwide prescriptive policies have little hope of altering classroom instruction in any predictable or systematic way.

It follows that changing a school requires changing the messages individual teachers and students get regarding their future classrooms. The education researchers Milbrey Wallin McLaughlin and Dale Mann have argued that if new school policies and programs are to succeed, they must be adopted simultaneously in a "critical mass" of classrooms within the same school, so that teachers and students know that their new efforts will not be ignored in future classrooms, as their students progress from one grade to the next.[4] The scope of change imagined by McLaughlin and Mann is quite large. Perhaps the biggest change in teacher and student expectations about their future treatment could be produced by creating completely new classrooms, when a school is emptied out and a new group of students and faculty are brought in to start over. Obviously, such changes are rare.

It is highly unlikely that teachers' and students' expectations for their future classrooms can be simply swept aside by new curriculum requirements, or by toughened teacher evaluations, or by most other school-reform policies. If students and teachers have pessimistic expectations about their future classrooms, then official promises and pronouncements will probably be irrelevant to them. Programs that affect only a small number of classrooms, and policies that do not substantially alter the classrooms that people will belong to in the future, are unlikely to influence the expectations—and thus the behavior—of teachers and students.

Such policies have little chance of improving schools. To be effective, education policies must produce real changes in teachers' and students' behavior, and must touch both their present and future classrooms.

Of course, school policies that directly change the daily lives of teachers and students—by hiring new teachers or changing students' classroom assignments, for example—will have powerful effects on their expectations for the future. Teacher hiring and classroom reassignments directly and powerfully change the classroom's membership, and thus change teachers' and students' daily experiences.

Schools can affect classrooms in other ways, too: principals provide important support to classrooms, which are the educational heart of the school; and the messages that schools send teachers and students about the future membership of their classrooms, through hiring and classroom assignments, matter a great deal to them. (These policy approaches are discussed in detail in part II.) Policies that support the work of people in classrooms, and that affect attendance, hiring, and classroom membership, will also raise teachers' and students' expectations about their future treatment. However, since there are great differences between classrooms in the same school, effective policies presumably will have to provide different kinds of support to each classroom. Smart principals know this already.

Vulnerability is the common strand that ties together all of the school policies that influence classrooms. It is vulnerability that causes teachers and students to pay attention to the school's sequence of classrooms, and to the future that their school holds for them. And it is the potential of school policies to alter teachers' and students' perceptions of their future vulnerability that can make school policies powerful,

by changing teacher hiring, classroom assignments, attendance, or by intervening in troubled classrooms. School policies that respond to teachers' and students' experiences of
vulnerability thus have the best chance to influence their
perceptions about the classrooms they will belong to in the
future.

PART II

Why Education Policies
Have Failed,
and How They Can Succeed

CHAPTER 6

Lessons from Bitter Experience:
The Laws of Education Policy

Most education policies attempt to improve student achievement by telling teachers and students how to do their work more successfully. The specific instructions they are given vary widely, but the approach is the same: a set of marching orders imposed on people in schools, in the belief that compliance with the new instructions will make the schools work better. The problem with these policies was summed up by the economist Harvey Averch and his associates in a study conducted for the President's Commission on School Finance: "Research has not identified a variant of the existing system that is consistently related to students' educational outcomes."[1] While schooling clearly contributes to students' achievement—children who go to school learn more than those who do not—there is no known school policy or program that consistently and predictably helps students learn more than any other school policy or program. In Averch's words:

The literature contains numerous examples of educational practices that seem to have affected students' outcomes. The problem is that there are invariably other studies, similar in approach and method, that find the same educational practice to be ineffective. And we have no clear idea of why a practice that seems to be effective in one case is apparently ineffective in another. . . . We must emphasize that we are not suggesting that nothing makes a difference, or that nothing "works." Rather, we are saying that research has found nothing that *consistently* and *unambiguously* makes a difference in students' outcomes.[2]

Unfortunately, this conclusion has not been contradicted by subsequent studies. Many other studies, including the largest empirical analysis of educational innovations, have found the same result.* Education policies have not worked. This chapter addresses the reasons for this failure, and introduces a new approach to education policy that can succeed.

Prescriptive Policies

The failure of education policies is due to the nature of the policies that have been tried: they attempt to improve education by enforcing particular instructional methods, curricula, and regulations on the people in schools; in other words, they prescribe how teachers and students are to go about the work of teaching and learning. All of them are based on the

---

*Paul Berman and Milbrey Wallin McLaughlin state that "No class of educational treatments has been found that consistently leads to improved student outcomes (when variations in the institutional setting and nonschool factors are taken into account)."[3] While the studies that found education policies to be ineffective were largely conducted in the 1970s, their conclusions have not been contradicted since that time. Instead, education research continues to avoid confronting the disturbing findings of Averch, Berman and McLaughlin, and others.

belief that education policies can only achieve their intended effects by prescribing teacher training, testing, books and materials, lesson plans and lesson time, teaching techniques, and compliance with official school policies. Prescriptive policies also contain a built-in way of responding to their own repeated failures: more prescriptions, in the form of so-called remedial programs, that for the most part repeat lessons that have previously failed to help low-achieving students. The dominant ideology of education policy is an ideology of prescription.

After prescriptive policies impose their mandates on people in schools, there is a great deal of monitoring, inspecting, and record-keeping to make sure that people are complying with the mandates (or at least appear to be complying). It is difficult to exaggerate the scope of prescriptive policies in schools; they touch every part of classroom life. They narrow teachers' and students' choices, create a repressive structure that enforces compliance with the prescribed policies, and spread the message that all of the school's classrooms should be the same—that is, all classrooms are told to follow the same prescriptions. Surprisingly, this approach is not at all controversial; it is accepted as the established norm in education. This abiding emphasis on educational prescriptions is deeply entrenched in the education policy debate.

Education policy has come to mean the issuing of prescriptions for local schools by the state and federal governments and by local school districts. The states determine which textbooks local schools can use; the rules for teacher licensing and evaluations of teachers; regulations on student discipline and suspensions; and more. The educational historian Diane Ravitch writes that the trend is increasingly for state legislatures to "tell teachers how to teach and what to teach."[4] The pattern has become so widespread and so intrusive that the education policy analyst Arthur Wise tagged it "legislated learning."[5] As for the federal government,

> Between 1964 and 1976, the number of pages of federal legislation affecting education increased from 80 to 360, while the number of federal regulations increased from 92 in 1965 to nearly 1,000 in 1977 . . . the number of federal court decisions affecting education numbered only 112 between 1946 and 1956, rose to 729 from 1956 to 1966, and climbed to "in excess of 1,200 in the next four years."[6]

Local school districts often prescribe teaching techniques, remedial programs, daily schedules, and the amount of "time on task" required for each subject of instruction. Prescriptive policies obsessively regulate every aspect of schooling. But as we have seen, they fail to improve student achievement.

These failures can be traced directly to the prescriptive nature of the policies: when prescriptive policies run up against the power of teachers and students to control events in their classrooms, the prescriptions are trounced. This suggests why prescriptive policies sometimes work for a short time, but never consistently: when a prescription happens to match the inclinations, strengths, and preferences of the people in a particular classroom, it has a good chance to be carried out and to help the people in that classroom do their work better. Without such a fortuitous match, the prescriptive policy collapses. In this sense prescriptive policies can sometimes succeed, yet they will ultimately fail to achieve sustained or consistent successes.

When a prescriptive policy tells teachers and students what to do and how to do it, the important differences among classrooms are ignored and even suppressed. Policy makers treat classroom differences as obstacles to the efficient execution of established prescriptive policies. If a teacher discovers a particularly effective way to teach a reading lesson and the official school district policy calls for a different method to be used, the teacher then must follow the rules or become an outlaw—and many teachers have felt forced to become outlaws.[7] Prescriptions ignore the ideas of teachers and students, the strengths and weaknesses they bring with them to school, and the unique evolution of teaching and learning in their classrooms. Teachers' and students' knowledge of each other and of their classrooms is treated as if it were useless. The possibility that teachers and students may discover successful methods of teaching and learning on their own is blithely cast aside by the prescriptive assumptions of the policy debate. The result has been policies that have failed to take into account the ways that teachers and students do their work, and thus have failed.

This pattern is so deeply established that it can be said to constitute the First Law of Education Policy:

> *Policies that prescribe teachers' and students' classroom activities do not produce sustained improvements in students' achievement. To be effective, education policies must give up the attempt to prescribe teachers' and students' actions.*[8]*

The record shows that prescriptive policies do not work in education: when a new prescriptive policy is introduced in a group of classrooms, the typical result will be that achievement levels will improve in a few classrooms, decline in a few classrooms, and show no change in most classrooms; in

---

*As Eric Hanushek has written, "the components of a successful school program are poorly understood, so there is no way to mandate an effective program by setting requirements on the educational process."[9]

follow-up studies the initial, temporary changes in achievement will gradually disappear.

It is important to be clear about what the First Law of Education Policy means: that *prescriptive* education policies do not improve student achievement. The First Law is of great importance precisely because the policy debate has been fixated on prescriptive policies, and has not considered other kinds of education policies. It is also important to notice that the First Law does *not* say that nothing works in education policy. The remainder of this book analyzes the little-known education policies that are *not* prescriptive, and therefore have a chance to succeed where conventional policies have failed.

Despite the First Law of Education Policy, policy makers' enthusiasm for prescriptive policies is apparently undiminished. They argue that prescriptive policies would work perfectly if only teachers and students would carry them out properly. In other words, the policies are fine, but the people in schools fail to live up to them. When the failure of past prescriptions is mentioned in the policy debate, it is cited as an indictment of old ideas; advocates of the latest educational prescriptions always believe that they have found the successful prescriptions that eluded their predecessors. The search for new prescriptive policies resembles the search for Atlantis, the lost continent; the fact that it has not yet been found does not prove its nonexistence; it might be discovered tomorrow. So the search continues, sustained by wishes and hopes, but not by evidence of consistent educational gains.

The prescriptive approach to education policy is now so entrenched and so widely accepted by all sides in the education policy debate that most simply assume education policies must necessarily be prescriptive policies. Even the writings of Arthur Wise, a thoughtful critic of prescriptive policies, assume that any "policy intervention" in education will be a prescriptive effort to "legislate" how teaching and learning will be carried out.[10] There are, however, alternatives to the prescriptive approach to education policy, as this chapter will show.

The Lessons of Policy Implementation

A clear and consistent finding of education policy research is that policies and reforms often fall apart when they encounter the realities of daily life in classrooms.[11] Education policy researchers call this "the implementation problem," but it is far more than that; it is a basic phenomenon deeply rooted in the workings of schools and classrooms. Because of the policy debate's obsession with prescriptive policies, little attention has been given to the question of why such a wide variety of prescriptive policies has suffered a uniformly discouraging fate; only a few research projects have tried to discover the reasons for the First Law of Education Policy. The largest of these was commissioned by the federal government in the 1970s, to find out whether the success rate of new education policies could be improved. Researchers at the Rand Corporation (including this book's author) were asked to look at the effects of finances, leadership, training, planning, and administration on education policies. The government wanted to examine the possibility that ineffective management was undermining education policies that were basically sound. The study produced a series of revelations, the most important of which was that classroom responses to the policies, rather than management failures, provided the crucial explanation for the fate of prescriptive policies.[12]

The study's principal researchers were Paul Berman, a political scientist who conducted the surveys and statistical analyses, and Milbrey Wallin McLaughlin, an education and evaluation specialist who led the field studies of schools. The research team visited 196 school districts in eighteen states, and carried out thousands of interviews. Their eight-volume report, *Federal Programs Supporting Educational Change* (better known as the Change Agent study) looked at a wide range of education policies and their effects. The Change Agent study team approached the problem of failed education policies by looking at the implemention process. Implementation refers to how education policies are carried out in each school and classroom: how a policy is planned, financed, introduced to principals and teachers, managed, and executed. At the core of the research was the insight that a policy's success depends not only on its educational techniques, but on the whole implementation process, beginning from the time the policy arrives at the front door of a school and continuing until it becomes part of the daily life of each classroom. According to this view, the same education policy might have completely different effects on different schools, depending on how the people in each school implemented it.[13] Other researchers up to this point had written about implementation, but none had studied its effects in such detail, or in so many different settings.

The Change Agent study's surveys found that innovative policies were carried out by different schools in many different ways; in fact, policies were carried out differently even among classrooms in the same school. The researchers found that

each classroom, each school, and each school system, being somewhat different from others, implements the same innovations in different ways at different times or places. In short, even when tested and developed at other sites, an educational innovation, unlike a new drug or a new variety of wheat, undergoes *adaptation* during implementation.[14]

The study concluded that every policy could be implemented in an infinite number of forms, with each classroom and school creating its own distinctive version of what were intended to be uniform policies. While principals, teachers, and students were putting a new policy into practice, they were altering and adjusting it.

The Change Agent surveys and field studies discovered that the process of implementation turns uniform prescriptions into extremely varied and often unrecognizable versions of the original policies. In education circles, this phenomenon is attributed to "the closed classroom door"—once teachers and students close the door to their classroom, they can behave in ways that ignore all the school's policy directives without being detected. A teacher gave this example of the closed classroom door:

> Curriculum coordinators dearly love to put out papers that say, We have now standardized the curriculum so that, across the board, [a particular curriculum is used]. And of course, that never *happens*.
>
> You can tell a teacher, "Do American History from 1600 to 1700"; [the teacher will say] "Okay, we'll cover it." But that's the most you can do. And the teacher will close the door, and do what they can do best. We'll cover, for example, certain irregular verbs, or certain biological processes, but everybody's going to do it in their own way.

What happens behind the closed classroom door is, of course, a result of reciprocal power in classrooms. This phenomenon has not caused policy makers to abandon prescriptive policies, but it has caused many school officials to admit to a sense of frustration and failure when their policies have been rejected by people in classrooms. For example, a well-known book about the job of the school principal quotes one principal as admitting, "I think sometimes they think it is easier just to close the door and get away from me—take this number of kids and just deal with them."[15]

The Change Agent study's detailed case studies of schools paints a compelling portrait of the implementation process.[16] At schools the researchers visited, there was a typical sequence of implementation, beginning with the introduction of the new policy and followed by the discovery of unanticipated difficulties, struggles among administrators and teachers, and then decisions (sometimes formal, sometimes informal) to make changes in the policy's goals and methods. Meanwhile, in their classrooms teachers and students were making their own changes in the policy and its officially-endorsed methods. When the researchers asked people to explain what happened after their school adopted a new policy, school officials and teachers repeatedly described a chain of events that altered and diversified the original plans. The events that triggered these policy changes were varied: sometimes the teaching materials didn't arrive on time, or didn't work as planned; sometimes certain parts of the policy seemed to work better than others, which then were abandoned; sometimes office politics undermined a new policy. There were always unforeseen events and unforeseen reactions from teachers and students that changed people's minds about how policies should be carried out. When students didn't respond as expected, teachers tried something different. Gradually these differences accumulated, and the policy took on a new form in each classroom. Teachers' and students' reciprocal power was imposing alterations on the classrooms in the Change Agent study.

Berman and McLaughlin searched for new words to describe the wrenching effects that implementation processes imposed on new education policies. They wrote that policies "mutated" as they were exposed to the rigors of schools and classrooms, and they referred to the "mutual adaptation" process through which policies were altered to conform to school practices, and vice versa.[17] Their careful descriptions of the evidence made it clear that policy prescriptions for teaching and learning simply were not being followed in the schools. They wrote, "Instead of the assured replication of transplanted projects, we found that the *same* innovation typically was implemented differently in different school districts, in different schools within the same school district, and even in different classrooms within the same school." There were major changes in prescribed teaching methods, in materials to be used in classrooms, even in the goals of the policies. Astonishingly, each classroom appeared to be able to change the policy in its own way. The Change Agent study examined education policies designed to prescribe and bring about specific changes in classroom behavior; instead, the policies were themselves subject to control by teachers and students. The evidence demonstrated that people in classrooms have more control over teaching and learning than do policy makers and school officials.[18]

The Change Agent study discovered that something unexpected was happening in classrooms during implementation—not just in a few scattered places, but in the vast majority—making it impossible for the research team to ignore the power of people in classrooms. This evidence that teachers and students adapt school policies to fit their classrooms' needs was the precursor of the analysis of reciprocal power presented in chapter 3.

As the Change Agent study's evidence on the transformation of policies by schools and classrooms accumulated, another study provided dramatic confirmation of its conclusions. The study was part of a social experiment set up to compare alternative methods of teaching five-year-olds in Head Start classes. In the Head Start Planned Variation experiment, eight carefully developed model programs were carried out in 167 classrooms in twenty-seven schools. Each of the models was developed by a team of experts who conducted the training, monitoring, and trouble-shooting for its own model. Because there were strongly motivated trainers and experts working with all the sites, it seemed likely that by the second year of the experiment, most classrooms would have achieved reasonably good implementation of their programs. Yet when the experts rated their own sites' teachers on their compliance with the program model, there were drastic differences between classrooms that were supposed to be carrying out the same program. Independent evaluators found the same result: the ostensibly standardized models had taken on different forms in each classroom; moreover, these changes had increased with the passage of time.[19] The author of the study, evaluation specialist Carol VanDeusen Lukas, concluded coolly that "classrooms under the same treatment label have differing experiences. . . . Moreover, all [eight] of the models changed during the course of the experiment."[20] In other words, even the most careful, well-financed and thorough implementation schemes resulted in drastic diversification and alteration of policies by the people in each classroom.

The research on implementation, which had begun with the hope of discovering ways to make education policies succeed, instead provided evidence that explained why policies have failed to have consistent effects on student achievement. This is not the first time that major social policy research has produced results that answered a question that its funders had not asked, but it is probably one of the more striking examples. The Change Agent researchers came up with convincing evidence that classroom variations were wrecking the prescriptive policies that are the heart of education policy in America. Its results, repeatedly confirmed by numerous other scholars, clearly deserve to be stated as the Second Law of Education Policy:

> *Policies applied to classroom activities are thoroughly reformulated by the actions of teachers and students in each classroom.*[21]

Teachers and students are able to reformulate education policies through their use of reciprocal power to control teaching and learning in their classroom, creating educational approaches that policy makers never foresaw. They will change a policy's methods of instruction, pace, use of materials, assignments, and even its goals. Consequently, any education policy—smaller classes, phonics instruction for reading, strict discipline, bilingual education, English immersion, computer-assisted instruction, or anything else—will take on a different and distinctive form in each classroom that implements it. By ignoring the ability of students and teachers to control what happens in their classrooms, education policy makers lose any realistic hope of learning how to influence events in classrooms. The idea that policy prescriptions can determine how teaching and learning are done simply turns out to be unrealistic.

Both the First and Second Laws of Education Policy point

to a reality the importance of which has yet to be accepted in the policy debate: *the effectiveness of education policies is completely dependent on the world of classrooms.* Indeed, it is now routine for teachers to admit their failure to comply with official school district policies. For example, a survey of seventy high school teachers in Philadelphia "found that the vast majority either ignored the [curriculum] mandates or adapted them to their own circumstances."[22] Teachers and students, not prescriptive policies, determine what happens in classrooms.

Pluralistic Policies

Prescriptive policies' record of failure suggests the need for a Third Law of Education Policy:

> *Education policies should be* designed *to achieve their effects despite being changed by the choices and responses of teachers and students.*[23]

It is to some extent an untested law, but one that is firmly based on the daily realities of life in classrooms. It calls for policies that are robust—that can stand up to all of the alterations that teachers and students impose on them—and that create new opportunities for improving education, and help people in classrooms take advantage of those opportunities in their own ways.

Most policy goals can be approached with either prescriptive or nonprescriptive methods, and the Third Law of Education Policy suggests that it is necessary for policy makers to give up tight administrative control in order to achieve educational results. Policy makers and school officials have not been able to make teaching and learning happen by issuing prescriptions for teachers and students to follow; the Third Law of Education Policy takes into account the realities of life and work in classrooms, and opens the way for thinking about policy from the point of view of teachers and students.

But is it possible to design an effective education policy that does *not* prescribe teachers' and students' actions? The idea of a nonprescriptive policy would strike most educators as a virtual contradiction in terms; abandoning prescriptions seems to require being disorganized and unsystematic. There are, however, many examples of education policies which, though little noticed, are nonprescriptive. Instead of telling teachers and students what to do, these policies are designed to take on different characteristics in each individual classroom. There are three somewhat overlapping types of nonprescriptive policies: incentives, deregulation, and what I call pluralistic policies, in which a wide variety of methods for reaching policy goals are encouraged and fostered.

Examples strongly suggesting that these approaches are capable of replacing education's prescriptive policies can easily be found in many policy arenas. In fact, nonprescriptive policies are all around us. The most obvious is the planned use of incentives to influence an individual's choices. Examples of incentives include reduced taxes on interest payments to encourage the purchase of homes, college scholarships for people who agree to serve in the military after they graduate, college scholarships for students who graduate from high school with a B average or better, and extra points in government contract competitions for companies that hire minority employees. The targets of these policies are not forced to behave in a particular way; instead, they are offered a voluntary exchange: the government will do something for them if they do something for the government. Incentive policies work when the government can offer an attractive deal in return for clearly specified actions on the part of the people targeted.

A second type of nonprescriptive policy is deregulation, or laissez-faire. Laissez-faire is a studied, intentional, planned government decision not to intervene in individuals' choices in the economy (or in some other area of governmental concern), and not to influence the economic structure that creates the choices that are available to individuals. Recent United States efforts to deregulate important publicly supported service industries (passenger air travel, truck freight transport, banking, telephone service, broadcasting, and notoriously, savings and loan institutions) are examples of the use of deregulation and laissez-faire policies. In some of these cases, deregulation was preceded by detailed studies and plans, including debates on the scope of the deregulation scheme, on transition arrangements, and on how the post-deregulation period should be monitored. (In the case of the deregulation of the savings and loans, this did not take place.) These examples of deregulation have not arisen through an absence of policy; they represent a coherent policy—a *nonprescriptive* policy—in their own right.

Both of these types of nonprescriptive policies, deregulation and incentives, have strengths and limitations. Deregulation encourages profit-seeking businesses to be creative and to adapt to clients' needs. Deregulation assumes that when clients are badly served, the marketplace will eliminate the offending businesses and encourage new ones to start up. However, such pressures to serve the public well may not exist in industries that have a lot of hard-to-serve clients. Some clients may be badly served because they live in remote, lightly populated markets, where deregulation has caused a reduction in bus and airline service. Others may suffer because conventional services do not work well for them, as is the case for many students from poor families, whom profit-making schools are not particularly anxious to serve. In these cases, deregulation may not produce desirable results, because it depends on the existence of a market in which hard-to-serve people have sufficient resources to purchase what they need.

Incentive policies have a weak spot that they, too, share with prescriptive policies: they aim to influence individuals to behave in a particular, predetermined way, eliciting specific actions from people who are offered a valued incentive. Despite their voluntary nature, incentives are a form of *dirigisme,* the old French strategy in which the government pointedly suggested to economic leaders precisely what they were expected to do. *Dirigisme* worked when the government was pointing in the right direction; in complicated or rapidly changing circumstances it was a disaster, because the government was usually pointing in the wrong direction. Incentive policies fail completely if the directions given by policy makers turn out to be wrong (as farmers discovered when they responded to government incentives to expand in the late 1970s; and all too often they have the effect of suppressing flexible adaptation to local circumstances.

In addition, incentives often can be perverted by clever responses that follow the letter but not the intent of the policy. In 1984, the state of California offered payments to local school districts that agreed to lengthen their school year; officials discovered that some districts were getting the money by lengthening the time for taking attendance, and adding one minute to the time between class periods—a brilliant response that was not, however, the goal of the incentive policy's designers.[24] Such undesirable responses make incentives ill-suited for solving most complicated policy problems, including many of those in education. Incentives depend on clarity and simplicity in the behavior they try to induce. Offering higher salaries to attract top college graduates into the teaching professsion is a clear and simple incentive policy; policies to create incentives for improving the reading achievement of poor students are not so easily designed or implemented.

A third kind of nonprescriptive policy, in widespread use but not recognized as the flexible and powerful strategy that it is, is the approach I choose to call pluralistic policy. Pluralistic policies are those that provide support for a diversity of problem-solving responses tailored to the needs and strengths of those most affected by the problems at hand. Here I would like to show how pluralistic policies differ from the prescriptive policies that have been used heavily in education. Later in this chapter and in chapters 7 and 8, I describe in detail pluralistic policies that offer the best chances to improve education.

Pluralistic policies have four parts:

- *They encourage diverse individual choices* by teachers, students, and parents as the principal means of solving problems. In this respect they resemble laissez-faire policies. Support for individual choices works by bringing together people who can work productively as a group, and then letting them do their work in their own ways. Some schools already provide for individual choices by teachers, students, and parents, taking advantage of their detailed knowledge about what they are good at, and allowing them to figure out for themselves what works educationally for them.*

---

*The economist Milton Friedman and his followers have proposed that students' and parents' choice of schools be facilitated by a system in which families would choose the school each student would attend. As I will argue in later chapters, the

- *They create new opportunities* from which individuals can choose, but without prescribing any one particular choice. This contradicts both the laissez-faire approach (which relies on the marketplace to create new choices) and the incentive approach (which pushes individuals toward making particular choices). New opportunities might include special programs offered in disadvantaged areas, greater involvement of teachers and principals in selecting new teachers for their school, subsidized transportation to reduce mid-year turnover of students in inner-city classrooms, services designed to encourage school attendance, and other options aimed at improving the quality of services available to hard-to-serve students.

- *They encourage each classroom to adapt its teaching and learning methods to its needs,* ignoring the prescriptive ideology's assumption that all classrooms should do things the same way. This means recognizing that the problems that arise in one classroom often are quite different from those in the classroom next door, and require solutions that are tailored to the needs of individual classrooms.

- *They provide shared support for the shared parts of the education system* such as teacher salaries, resources to deal with learning disabilities, and the schools' physical plant, buses, cafeterias, financing, and capital planning. This avoids deregulation's tendency to abandon poor communities.

Pluralistic education policies influence classroom teaching and learning without creating new rules, required methods of instruction, or prescriptive programs. Instead, they aim to improve student achievement by determining the classroom's

---

choice of a student's *school* ignores the more important issue of the *classroom within the school* to which the student is assigned. Thus, policies permitting school choice may do little to match students and teachers with the educational settings in which they will be most productive.[25]

membership, by providing organized support for the efforts of people in classrooms to improve teaching and learning, by stimulating diversity, and by creating mechanisms for interventions in failing classrooms. Crucially, they use policy levers that are not prescriptions for specific methods of teaching and learning. What is perhaps most important about these policies is that they already exist. They are now a small, relatively neglected part of education policy, but they offer major lessons for the future.

One thing is clear: all policies that determine a classroom's membership—by changing students' classroom assignments, or recruiting new teachers—already have a powerful and direct impact on teaching and learning, without prescribing methods of instruction.* For example, school policies currently determine whether students who are disrupting a classroom can be moved to another class. Policy decisions also are responsible for the placement of novice teachers (whose inexperience reduces their effectiveness[27]) in schools with many low-achieving students; this pattern often results from rules negotiated between school management and teachers' unions.[28] A school district's policies for assigning novice teachers can affect classrooms dramatically, even though such policies do not prescribe particular teaching methods. In general, students' classroom assignments and the recruiting of new teachers are given little attention by policy makers and are handled mechanically, because they have not been important issues in the education policy debate. Still, these policies and others that directly influence the membership of

---

*In his careful analysis of empirical research on student achievement, Richard Murnane concludes that "The primary resources that are consistently related to student achievement are teachers and other students. Other resources affect student achievement primarily through their impact on the attitudes and behaviors of teachers and students."[26]

classrooms are vitally important (although rarely discussed) in the universe of education policies. While prescriptive policies have had little effect on classroom events, assignment and recruiting policies influence classrooms every day. (These and other classroom membership policies are discussed in detail in chapters 7 and 8.)

The relationship between school principals and their teachers also can be a nonprescriptive source of improvement in teaching and learning.[29] Instead of being the enforcer of prescriptive policies, the principal can reorganize his or her activities to provide support to classrooms—support that leaves important choices about teaching and learning up to teachers and students.[30] Support from the principal implicitly aims to help people in classrooms accomplish their goals independently of prescribed procedures: the principal responds to the needs expressed by teachers and students, and thereby helps them to get on with their work. There are already many principals who provide flexible support to classrooms in their schools; but education policies have neither supported nor even acknowledged their efforts.

The most obvious kinds of support that principals can give to classrooms are resources: small allocations of money, materials, and books; permission to use the auditorium stage for a class play; extra pay for the sponsors of student activities. The principal's support can also take the form of suggestions, encouragement, and listening to problems. Principals have the power to lift restrictive rules that constrain teacher and student activities; this form of support is sometimes symbolic, since the people in a classroom often can ignore the rules once the classroom door is closed, but it is still valued by teachers and students. In some school districts, principals can arrange for training and referrals for teachers in response to their requests for assistance with specific classroom problems.[31] Even something as simple as making sure students are in their classrooms rather than loitering in corridors is a way for principals to provide support for teaching and learning.[32] Clearing the halls has several functions: it stabilizes the membership of the school's classrooms, adds a few minutes to the time available for classroom work (extra time that becomes significant when added up over a year), and provides particular support for the necessary "housekeeping" activities in classrooms, such as taking attendance. Principals' support helps people in classrooms get on with the work of teaching and learning; but it requires the principal to recognize, accept, and support the differences among classrooms, which is not allowed by prescriptive policies that require uniformity and compliance. (Additional policies for providing support to classrooms are described in chapter 7.)

Perhaps the most difficult problem that principals face is knowing how to provide support that actually improves teaching and learning in an ineffective classroom. When principals (and others, such as reading specialists) provide support to teachers, they tend to maintain the classroom's existing patterns of behavior, and avoid drastic changes.[33] This approach to providing support is realistic and pragmatic, but also limited in what it can accomplish; it relies on existing classrooms and classroom relationships, even when they are problematic. Such an approach has a clear cost: if teachers and students don't want to be in their current classrooms, and don't want to put their energy into teaching and learning, then support from the principal or the reading specialist is unlikely to improve their work.

In situations where classroom problems are too severe to respond to support and assistance from the principal or from other teachers, interventions may be effective—but not by imposing educational prescriptions on the failing classroom. Teachers and students will use their reciprocal power to resist the imposition of policy prescriptions when things are going badly in their classroom just as much as when things are going well. If people in a classroom have learned from each other that serious efforts to teach and learn will be greeted with hostility and ridicule, then prescriptions from school officials are not likely to change their minds.[34] The interventions that are most likely to succeed may require changing the classroom's membership: breaking up groups that resist the teacher, reassigning students to a teacher with whom they can work, or switching teachers between classrooms.

What happens with us is, if a class goes bonkers, it's changed. It's split. This year, a junior English class just didn't work. It was just off the walls. This was a very good, experienced teacher, too. It just didn't work; bad chemistry. The class was broken up, in mid-October, when it was quite clear that it just wasn't going to fly. And this was a teacher experienced enough to try a number of things.

The core of the class was broken up into two different classes; the ones who'd gotten along well with the original teacher [were] left with her; some of them reassigned to other classes; a housemaster picked up the others. The group that had given the most trouble was completely split among five different classes by the time it was all over.

These things aren't done lightly; the head of the English department, two guidance counselors, the teacher and the housemaster were all involved. Some of the kids were asked who they'd like to have. And they were listened to. Since I've been here, which has been for five years, I've seen at least four classes just disbanded and reorganized like this, so it's not particularly rare for us.

Rearranging the membership of a failing classroom is a radical intervention, but notice that it is not a *prescription* for how the new classroom is supposed to do its work. Instead, it uses the principal's leverage to set up new classroom relationships, and relies on the new combinations of teachers and students to design the work of teaching and learning—which only they can do.

Another nonprescriptive policy for dealing with existing classrooms that are performing poorly is an official school policy that allows teachers and students to choose the educational approach that they want to follow. Magnet schools and special-interest programs attract teachers and students with a common interest, and often allow them considerable freedom to shape their own classroom's work. These "schools of choice" represent another approach that drastically changes classroom events without attempting to control teachers' and students' behavior.*

What these nonprescriptive policies have in common is their reliance on people in classrooms, rather than prescriptive policies, to manage the day-to-day substance of teaching and learning. They use recruiting and classroom assignments to improve teachers' and students' performances. They provide official support tailored to fit the needs of individual classrooms, rather than attempting to suppress classroom differences. They accept the choices and actions of teachers and students, and provide mechanisms (magnet schools and other self-directed programs) for those choices to be used productively. At times of classroom failure, they allow for interven-

---

*The California Business Roundtable proposed a plan in 1988 for reforming the state's schools, including the introduction of programs of school choice within the public school system for all high-school students.[35] While some elements of the plan were not accepted by the state education department, there may be a test of public school choice for children three to six years old.

tions that aim to remove the main sources of problems while giving teachers and students the responsibility for making needed improvements. Nonprescriptive policies attempt to control only those parts of schooling that are not controlled by classrooms; they recognize that people in classrooms control education, and only use policies to determine membership and to provide support for classrooms. The alternative, as the record of prescriptive policies has revealed, is to try to control what cannot be controlled—and to invite the failures that inevitably follow from that effort.

As an example of a pluralistic policy in education, consider the following hypothetical case: A local school district's officials decide to establish a new magnet junior high school. They select the school's principal, instructing her to recruit *voluntarily* her faculty from existing schools in the district, and to develop the school's program in cooperation with the new faculty. She is then to recruit students to attend the school. The principal and her faculty decide to give the school a health sciences focus, and they scour libraries for ideas to use in their classrooms. They attract students (and parents) by advertising the school's offerings, its methods, and its faculty members. Notice that the initial policy decision to establish the school triggers the creation of new choices and opportunities for teachers, parents, and students. Those who become members of the school do so because they have decided that they want to work there.

After the school opens, let us assume there are problems, signalled by low test scores, staff turnover, and dissatisfaction expressed by parents, teachers, or students. The principal, still relatively free from prescriptions imposed by the local school authorities, pursues a mixed strategy to solve the school's problems. She arranges to transfer students (and perhaps teachers as well) who are having difficulties to different classrooms. In other classrooms where teachers and students are having difficulties, she arranges for training to respond to teachers' questions and needs, and perhaps for assistance from specialists to help teachers deal with particular students. She recruits new teachers to fill the gaps in her school's offerings. For each classroom problem, she works out a solution tailored to the particular circumstances in that classroom. She intervenes only when turnover, low achievement, or dissatisfaction indicate a problem; otherwise, she encourages teachers and students to adapt the school's program to their own circumstances.

In subsequent years, she increases the choices available to teachers and students by establishing a system in which students receive their first or second choice of teachers for most of their classes. Students and teachers are in classrooms that they have chosen, in which they can succeed; if they do not, a transfer to another classroom is considered. She then responds to under- and over-subscribed classes with more teacher training and targeted recruitment of new teachers. Teachers adapt their classrooms to their students, using books, materials, and methods of instruction in their own ways, without worrying about district rules. To complete the example, let us assume that the principal's efforts to recruit the best teachers receive the district's support, in the form of higher teacher salaries.

Of course, this is a radically simplified example. What is important is that it contains all of the raw materials of pluralistic policy: the encouragement of active and diverse individual choices by both teachers and students; official action to establish new educational choices; interventions tailored to the specific circumstances of each classroom problem; and shared support for common problems. Not only do teachers and students decide in which school and classroom they want to work; the pluralistic policies also allow them to figure out methods of teaching and learning that are effective for them, and to change those methods as necessary, even if it means that different approaches are used in adjacent classrooms in the same school. These may range from lectures to student-directed approaches, the use of varied textbooks and materials, and teacher-designed assignments and homework. In cases of classroom failure, the principal's interventions are pluralistic, responding differently to each classroom's problems.

The strategy that lies behind pluralistic policies essentially is one of providing many different routes to the goal of student achievement—one for each classroom. The beauty of pluralistic policies is that they are flexible even within classrooms, reflecting the fact that what works for one student may not for another. Trial and error—and reciprocal power—can be used to the benefit of each student. In the magnet school example, the ability of teachers and students to choose their classrooms improves the chances that they will be successfully matched with an educational program that meets their needs, as does the possibility of switching people to different classrooms if their initial assignments don't work well. In addition, encouraging variation among the magnet school's classrooms strengthens the school's adaptation to its students. This approach also provides the people in charge of a school with early warnings about problems: staff turnover, recruitment difficulties, over- and under-subscription are clear signals that different kinds of support are needed by at least some of the school's classrooms.

Pluralistic policies require that many crucial educational decisions must be worked out by teachers and students. What is gained is the opportunity to take advantage of the differences among teachers, among students, and among classrooms: pluralistic policies stimulate classrooms to use educational methods tailored to their own particular members. Other policy approaches, such as prescriptions, centralized incentive systems, and even deregulation, ignore those differences. By encouraging a wide variety of ways to solve educational problems, pluralistic policies give every classroom a chance to succeed.

The set of strategies I have referred to as pluralistic policy is the result of applying classical pluralist political thought to the realm of policy design. The philosophical basis for pluralism, according to the political philosopher Isaiah Berlin, is that there are important differences among human beings that make it appropriate to allow them to devise diverse and individualized solutions to their problems.[36] Another strand of pluralist thinking is essentially empirical. The legendary theorist Harold Laski and other turn-of-the-century British writers argued that in Western nations, the idea of the sovereign, all-controlling state does not accurately describe reality. They pointed out that society is made up of groups that engage every day in making choices that govern their own lives and that have important consequences for the rest of society.[37] Taken together, these small units are more able to invent and apply new ideas, more flexible, and more error-tolerant than any centralized, prescriptive social order possibly could be. In this reading, the genius of pluralism is its ability to produce results in highly diverse, difficult, complicated situations.

I would suggest that education fits both of these strands of thought. Philosophically (and educationally), it is desirable to encourage people in individual classrooms to design effective methods of solving the problems they confront there; empirically, there appears to be no viable alternative to allowing them to do so.

Pluralistic policies already exist in education, despite their incompatibility with the ideology of prescription. When school principals encourage their teachers to adapt the official curriculum to their classrooms' particular circumstances, they are inventing their own pluralistic policy. When guidance counselors, teachers, and principals arrange to transfer a student who is having difficulty to another classroom where he or she can work more effectively, pluralistic policy is being used. The daily reality of pluralistic practice is demonstrated by the whole range of ad hoc alterations constantly being made in local school practices, by pragmatic principals and teachers who have learned to bend the rules to accommodate the diversity they find in their classrooms every day. They have learned what works and what doesn't. The Rand Corporation's study of twenty inner-city Los Angeles schools found that achievement gains were higher where teachers were encouraged to adapt or modify their schools' reading program on an individual classroom basis.[38]

The pluralistic policies described here are not alien to the schools. However, the prevailing ideology of prescriptive policy often transforms nascent pluralistic policies into prescriptive ones. For example, some magnet schools have gradually lost their power to recruit their own teachers, as part of district plans to "streamline" the personnel process— clearly a centralized, prescriptive policy. Such changes can replace the adaptability of pluralistic policies with central-office prescriptions. The crucial point is that the effectiveness of pluralistic policies does not come from a label that reads "magnet school" or "school-based management;" it comes from the ability of people in schools to replace prescriptive ideology with policies that take advantage of the inherent variation among classrooms, and encourage a diversity of solutions to classroom educational problems.

CHAPTER 7

Policies That Take
Classrooms Seriously

THE file of education policies capable of getting results by controlling classroom events has been shown to be empty. By contrast, educational research literature is full of classroom events that have dominated official policies. The following examples underscore the fact that teachers' and students' choices determine how their classrooms work. Their choices interact with education policies to create educational results:

- In a Northeastern urban high school where attendance is a top policy priority, daily absentee rates in 1988 rose steeply, to levels over 20 percent.[1] The choice of many students not to come to school amounts to a kind of near-dropping-out. Absenteeism is even higher in numerous other American high schools; what is striking about the example is its demonstration of the failure of get-tough attendance policies.

- The psychologists Esther and Seymour Sarason studied the New Math curriculum of the 1960s in a sample of upper-middle-class suburban schools.[2] The New Math used methods of logical proof, student discovery, and analysis to teach mathematics—approaches that were wholly absent from the observed classrooms. The new curriculum had itself been changed by teachers and students. They imposed their old, familiar classroom relationships and study methods on the New Math, creating an amalgam of ideas and techniques not envisioned or understood by the designers of the new curriculum or by local school officials.

- Milbrey McLaughlin's study of educational evaluations found that teachers often resisted or refused to comply with official requests for classroom information.[3] Instead, they submitted reporting forms full of lengthy comments and information different from what had been requested. This resulted in data that were essentially useless, and the evaluations were ruined. Without the teachers' decision to cooperate with the data-gathering effort, it was doomed.

- The Change Agent study (discussed in chapter 6) found that people in classrooms altered and reformulated the innovations they were supposed to implement. Individual classrooms changed the materials, instructional techniques, assigned activities, and the roles of teachers and students; everything that could be changed, was changed.*

These examples and many others demonstrate the power of teachers' and students' choices over the events in their classrooms.

---

*Berman and McLaughlin summarize their findings: "Implementation—rather than the adoption of a technology, the availability of information about it, or the level of funds committed to it—dominates the innovative process and its outcomes."[4]

Teachers' and Students' Choices

Teachers and students determine the effects of school policies in two ways. One is through their use of reciprocal power to achieve a direct impact on daily classroom events (as earlier chapters have shown). The other way is through their power to make choices that determine the membership of particular schools and classrooms; these choices, too, drastically influence the effects of education policies. What happens is that many individual teachers, students, and parents decide which schools they prefer, and act on their decisions by transferring, moving, or (in the case of teachers) accepting a job offer in a desirable school. These individual decisions, when added together, affect later choices made by others, who choose a school based on the teachers and students already there. The local school district's rules on how teachers and students will be assigned to schools have significant effects, but the rules fall far short of controlling teachers' and families' behavior and choices. Teachers decide for themselves whether to apply for a position in a particular school district, and whether to accept the school and classroom assignment offered. They compare job opportunities in teaching and in other kinds of work, and can keep searching until they find an acceptable choice.* Parents choose where to live based in part on the quality of public schools, and pay substantially more for housing that enables their children to attend desirable schools, as economists David Grether and Peter Mieszkowski have shown.[6] Because low-income families are less able to choose

---

*Richard Murnane and Randall Olsen refer to teaching's "opportunity cost" as the increase in earnings a teacher would receive if he or she switched to an occupation other than teaching; this increment is the opportunity the teacher forgoes by continuing to teach—and therefore can be seen as the "opportunity cost" to a teacher remaining in the teaching profession.[5]

schools by means of their housing decisions, often their children are sorted into schools according to their economic circumstances. A community's school-enrollment pattern is thus the result of the accumulated choices and actions of families that can afford to choose their housing and families that cannot. Taken together, parents' and teachers' choices, made in response to the official school-assignment rules but not controlled by them, determine the membership of each school.

Because the distribution of teachers and students to schools is determined ultimately by the choices of teachers, students, and parents, the membership of schools is a result of what economists call *self-selection*. Self-selection happens through teachers', students', and parents' choices of residential location, school programs, school transfers, daily attendance decisions, and (for teachers) job choices.[7] The process of self-selection is one in which teachers and families respond to their options and to the official school-assignment rules, figuring out for themselves how to get into the school they want. Self-selection by families that have moved into desirable school zones and by teachers who have obtained desirable and secure teaching jobs, affects the opportunities open to others by determining what is available for them. Both the official assignment rules *and* teachers' and students' self-selection are important influences on schools. In the end, however, the power is with the thousands of choices made by teachers and families that, taken together, determine who goes to each school and classroom.

Since the membership of a classroom strongly and directly affects everything that happens there, the self-selection process is inevitably a powerful determinant of the effects of education policies. Reciprocal power rules the classroom, and classroom membership determines whose reciprocal power will be used there.

The fact that school effectiveness is drastically affected by the actions of teachers, students, and families is widely known among education policy specialists. It usually is interpreted as evidence of the limits on the effectiveness of education policies. However, these choices are much more than a set of limitations on policy; they demonstrate the control exerted by teachers and students over what happens in schools. Teachers' and students' self-selection decisions determine the membership of schools and classrooms; their reciprocal power governs the events that take place within each classroom. Self-selection and reciprocal power—the products of choices by teachers, students, and families—are the major, but rarely acknowledged, determinants of education. The basic facts of who will take part in education and how they will carry out the work of teaching and learning are, in the end, controlled by the decisions of teachers and students.

This description of the shared power of teachers and students makes it possible to go beyond the first three laws of education policy, which describe the bitter lessons of policies' inability to control education; it is now possible to explain what actually makes education policies work, in the Fourth Law of Education Policy:

The consequences of an education policy are determined by the choices of teachers and students.[8*]

In other words, a policy's effectiveness depends on the decisions and behavior of teachers and students. Notice that

*As Richard Murnane writes, "The central school resources—teachers and students—will respond to any changes in the institutional rules, customs, or contract provisions that determine the allocation of resources. Some of these behavioral responses will enhance student achievement; others will diminish achievement. The nature of the responses will depend on the priorities and opportunities of these key actors."[9]

the key role is played by their observed choices, and not by their opinions; elementary-school students may not talk at length about education policies, but their behavior still determines the consequences of new policies in their classrooms.

It follows from the Fourth Law that for an education policy to affect teaching and learning, it must influence the behavior of teachers and students, either by shaping their self-selection choices or by altering their classroom behavior. Policies that do one or both of these things have a chance to achieve an effect on classroom events, and thus on students' education. Those that do not affect teachers' and students' self-selection choices, or their classroom behavior, have little chance to influence student achievement.

The problem of finding policies that can influence teachers' and students' choices is a difficult one; most education policies have not even attempted to solve it. Instead of taking account of teachers' and students' choices and figuring out how to influence them, education policies have been based on the assumption that they can direct and control teachers' and students' behavior. When this failed, they were powerless to improve students' education. As one school district superintendent put it, "You can tell teachers what the policy is, but ultimately it's up to them." Designing effective education policies thus requires piecing together the scattered evidence on policies that influence teachers' and students' choices, rather than trying (and inevitably failing) to dominate them.

The existing educational research literature provides firm ground for the laws of education policy; however, the research on policies that recognize teachers' and students' choices so far is only suggestive. Based on the description of classrooms presented here, the most likely ways for policies to improve schooling can be summed up in the Policy Effectiveness Hypothesis:

> *The greatest impacts on teaching and learning will be produced by policies that change teachers' and students' classroom membership and policies that lead teachers and students to decide to change their classroom behavior.*

According to this view, policies can improve schools by taking advantage of the power of self-selection by teachers and students, and by taking advantage of the diversity and creativity of classroom reciprocal power. Instead of ignoring or attempting to overpower the choices of teachers and students, policies should recognize and use the ideas and energies of the people in each classroom.

Classroom Membership Policies

Every policy that influences the membership of a school or classroom, that is, every policy that affects its teachers' and students' decisions to be there, their decisions on how long to stay, and their decisions on how often to attend, affects the school's classrooms and the teaching and learning that take place there. Several kinds of policies affect classroom membership:

- policies governing the *assignment and reassignment* of teachers and students to schools and classrooms;
- policies relating to the daily school *attendance* of teachers and students, and the *turnover* of classroom enrollments;
- policies aimed at *recruiting* teachers and students to schools and classrooms (including teacher salary policies);

• policies designed to facilitate teachers' and students' *choices among schools and classrooms.*

While the policies covered in this list are varied, they are all pluralistic policies, because they do not prescribe a specific method of education; they make it possible for people in different classrooms to pursue their own approaches to teaching and learning effectively.

Assignment and reassignment policies. When school officials draw up classroom rosters, they take many factors into account, including the complicated scheduling requirements of high-school classes, the tracking of students into groups with similar achievement levels, students' course selections, and in some cases, information on which students are likely to benefit from a particular classroom or teacher. Classroom-assignment policies have a direct impact on the membership of every classroom in a school. Predicting which students will do best in a given classroom or which teacher is best suited to teach a given student is no easy task for school officials, but that is no reason to ignore it as a policy issue. When a school district's established personnel procedures assign novice teachers to schools whose average student-achievement levels are low (as now happens in many places), they are using teacher-assignment policies in a way that damages the education of disadvantaged students. When computer-generated student classroom assignments are held as sacrosanct, even when students and teachers present plausible cases for changing them, an opportunity for matching students with the most appropriate classrooms is being missed. Classroom assignment policies constantly shape teaching and learning, but only rarely are used to *enhance* teaching and learning.

Even if there are great difficulties in using assignment policies to match teachers and students with the classrooms for which they are best suited, there is no reason to leave manifest errors of the current system uncorrected. Classroom *reassignments*—that is, transfers to other, more suitable classrooms—should be made far easier than they are today. When a student is not learning, the strongest response is not to assign that student to a remedial program for an hour each day, but to place the student in a different classroom, with different classmates and a different teacher, thereby changing the system of reciprocal power that governs the student's work. There are no guarantees of success when such a change is made; but neither are there guarantees for remedial programs. What is certain, though, is that changing a student's classroom assignment is the biggest change in the daily opportunities to learn that a school can provide.[10] If school officials can take advantage of the process of matching teachers and students to classrooms, they will thereby have increased the effectiveness of the school—without spending additional money.

Increasing the priority placed on classroom assignment and reassignment policies, for both teachers and students, also will encourage school officials to pay increased attention to information on teachers' and students' individual strengths and needs when making classroom assignment decisions.

When teachers and students themselves know what kinds of classrooms (with what classmates and what activities) are best suited for them, that information should be used in the assignment process. One way to take advantage of that information would be for school officials to ask teachers and students to choose classrooms to which they want to be assigned. (Such policies are discussed in detail in the next chapter.)

Classroom assignment and reassignment policies have a

direct and immediate impact on the membership of every classroom; they influence everything that happens in every classroom they touch. Without imposing the slightest prescription on how a teacher will teach, or how students will learn, assignment policies shape the basic classroom membership, whose use of reciprocal power will control the classroom. The educational importance of classroom membership policies makes them the most powerful and attractive way for school officials, teachers, students, and parents to use their influence to improve the performance of the education system.

Attendance and turnover. The membership of a classroom is not permanently fixed in September; in an important sense, it is subject to the choices made every day by teachers and students about whether to go to school that day. If a teacher or student is absent from class, he or she will miss the day's events, its work, and its episodes of classroom reciprocal power. The absent person is lost to the classroom, and is beyond the reach of its educational activities.

Policies that improve teacher and student attendance can thus strengthen the effectiveness of their classroom. A salary bonus for teachers' unused sick days (on a scale negotiated with the teachers' union, to protect against potential abuses) could be beneficial in schools with many days of teacher absences. However, teacher absences are also a strong signal of their dissatisfaction, and of a lack of official support for classrooms, which should trigger strong management action to identify and respond to these problems. Teacher absences are thus a potential target for policy action, and a warning of deeper problems to which officials should attend.

Student attendance problems have a wide range of causes, including family problems, school failure, the attractions of street life, and dissatisfaction with their classrooms. To be effective, policies aimed at improving student attendance should provide accurate and timely information on which students are absent, followed by quick action tailored to the needs of each absent student. Policies can be drawn from a repertoire that includes automated telephone calls to parents, home visits, teacher conferences, reassigning the student to another classroom, or finding an appropriate referral to social or family services. These policies can improve students' attendance, and thus their learning, without prescribing educational methods to be used in their classroom. Yet even these policies will fail to improve attendance if the classroom to which the student returns does not provide stimulating and engaging teaching and learning.* School officials therefore should determine whether student absenteeism is a red flag signaling classroom problems that require an intervention or a reassignment.

Attendance problems are not the only cause of day-to-day changes in a classroom's membership. The classroom's membership also is disrupted when students change schools as a result of a mid-year family residential move. Some classrooms have so much turnover in their membership during the school year that there are thirty or more exits and new enrollments in the course of a year—more new students than the classroom's total enrollment at any one time. Turnover undermines the processes of reciprocal power that gradually build up a classroom's methods of education. It even lowers the achievement of students who are *not* mobile, but who are affected by the comings and goings of classmates.[12] Students who migrate from school to school as their parents move

---

*Policies aimed at improving attendance were recently found to fail in New York City because they did not address the quality of classrooms to which students returned.[11]

within a city lose the sustained teaching and learning relationships they need, and their entries and departures interrupt the established relationships of their classmates and teachers. Classroom turnover harms teaching and learning, but education policies have ignored this fact.

The most neglected student-attendance policies are those that would be required to keep a school's membership stable throughout the year. If schools offered subsidized bus transportation and strong encouragement for students to finish the school year in their original school, teaching and learning would benefit appreciably. Designing new policies to boost student attendance and to keep classroom memberships stable would build significant opportunities to improve education pluralistically, without prescribing how people in classrooms are supposed to do their work. Policies on attendance and turnover lack the surface appeal of such obviously "educational" policies as textbook selection and curriculum design, and are unlikely to attract the media coverage that curriculum disputes receive. They may, however, have more impact on classroom membership, and thus on educational results.

Recruiting. A school's recruiting policies, for both teachers and students, are impossible to separate from the work that takes place in classrooms, because recruitment determines classroom membership—and the people who are present in each classroom determine what will happen there. Yet the education policy debate treats teacher recruitment as if it were merely an administrative problem of filling empty job slots, and has largely ignored the problem of recruiting students to public schools that they view as desirable and effective. Overlooking the importance of teacher and student recruiting has caused policy makers to miss a superb opportunity for building effective classrooms.

Successful recruiting policies begin with teacher salaries that are high enough to attract intellectually able and energetic college students away from other opportunities. There is clear and compelling evidence that unattractive salaries discourage people who want to become teachers from entering and staying in teaching.[13] School districts simply cannot recruit college graduates who have other job offers unless they offer competitive salaries. Moreover, former teachers (including women who left teaching at the time their children were born) also are influenced in their decision on whether to reenter teaching by the salaries that are offered in teaching, as compared to other jobs. Like it or not, schools must compete with other employers if they are to recruit skilled and energetic teachers.

Effective teacher recruitment also requires that school personnel officials actively seek out the best new and returning teachers, handle their applications speedily, and help them find schools that will support and encourage them. Unfortunately, many school district personnel offices discourage more good applicants than they recruit—by their inefficiency, delays, impersonal treatment, and by ignoring requests for assignments to particular schools.[14] This chronic crisis will only change when policy makers make it their business to reform school personnel operations.

Teacher recruiting also is affected by the attractiveness of the job itself. According to interviews with teachers, attractive teaching jobs are those that provide collaboration and assistance from other teachers, as well as working conditions that allow teachers to respond in a sustained way to the needs of their students[15] (for example, through high school classes of longer duration than the fifty minute norm).

Public school officials often think that they do not need to recruit students. The benefit of doing so, however, is that they will increase the number of students who enroll because those students are well-matched to the school's programs. Some school officials think it impossible to recruit public-school students—but as we have seen, there are many families that decide where to live based on the local schools. For students (and their parents), successful recruiting requires that schools offer skilled and energetic teachers, and be willing to adapt to students' strengths and needs. Recruiting students means marketing a school's educational opportunities to them, and then delivering those opportunities by offering desirable classes, safe facilities, opportunities to learn, and support for every classroom. Once students are recruited—that is, once they have decided that they *want* to be part of a particular school and classroom—other school issues are more easily resolved; attendance, for example.

Recruiting students and teachers may seem to be an obvious way to improve education, but recruiting strategies fall between the cracks of the current education policy debate. Recruiting fits neither the conservative program of stricter controls nor the liberal program of more resources and services. The policy debate's rhetoric encourages school people to focus their attention on pedagogy and curriculum, rather than on recruiting teachers and students and allowing them to figure out teaching and learning for themselves. Recruiting policies are pluralistic, unlike the prescriptive education policies with which the policy debate is most familiar; if widely used, they will foster a diversity of classroom approaches to education.

Only one major policy proposal takes recruiting completely seriously: the magnet school (sometimes called the alternative school). Magnet schools typically are located in poor and minority neighborhoods, and offer special school programs to attract a racially integrated enrollment from both nearby and distant neighborhoods. As a means to achieving their goal of desegregation, magnet schools engage in a great deal of recruiting. Notice that magnet schools recruit not only students but teachers as well; and students and teachers who are attracted to a magnet educational program are willing to devote extraordinary energy to make it work. When Anthony Alvarado and Sy Fliegel were in charge of public schools in New York City's East Harlem neighborhood, from 1974 to 1984, they established over twenty "theme schools" offering special programs in science, communications, ecology, art, and other fields. Every school in the district became a theme school, and was given responsibility for attracting teachers and students, as well as for choosing its own methods, materials, and books. "The big thing introduced here was teachers' choice, not parental choice," said Deborah Meier, one of the first alternative-school principals in the district. There are now more than thirty theme schools and minischools in the East Harlem community school district, created by the teachers and staff of that district's schools. In ten years, the achievement scores of the district's overwhelmingly poor and minority enrollment improved dramatically. The schools succeeded because they recruited teachers and students whose choices led them to work together effectively.[16] For magnet and alternative schools, recruiting teachers and students is a way of matching what they offer to the people who want those offerings. Other public schools can do the same thing, if they so desire.

Most school districts apply a policy of reverse recruiting to their inner-city schools: they offer skilled, senior teachers the opportunity to transfer to less demanding jobs working with more affluent, easier-to-teach students, and make few efforts to retain them in the schools whose students need them most. The effect of reverse recruiting has been described by the economists David Greenberg and John McCall: the most desirable schools in a district gradually acquire its most experienced teachers, while the least desirable schools—typically containing the hardest-to-teach students—are staffed by the district's novice teachers.[17] Reverse recruiting policies insure that even if a district has special programs to help its low-achieving students, the teachers who are part of those programs will be relatively inexperienced and in a state of constant turnover. It would be difficult to imagine a situation more likely to undermine the education received by poor children. Instead of recruiting skilled and experienced teachers to inner-city schools by offering them opportunities to collaborate with other teachers, desirable working conditions, and the chance to build programs suited to their strengths and their students' needs, most school districts do little or nothing to retain them in the inner city, with predictable results. Instead of designing policies that use teachers' and students' self-selection to strengthen inner-city schools (as do magnet schools), they use teachers' self-selection decisions to undermine those schools. This example suggests that the opportunities posed by self-selection have not yet been tapped by the schools.

Choices among schools and classrooms. There is one more classroom-membership policy, one that uses the information possessed by students and parents to alter the membership of classrooms. That policy is to make the choices of students and their families the basis for assigning students to classrooms. (The specific details of this policy are discussed in chapter 8.) When school districts and schools adopt policies that recognize student choice as a factor in school and classroom assignments, they shift membership policies away from the control of school officials and toward students. However, so far the shift has been very limited. Most existing choice plans involve only the choice of the school (or minischool) a student will attend; *classroom* choice is a rarity in American education. Where school choice exists, it is modified by other policies: desegregation requires ethnic balancing; fairness for all applicants may require a selection lottery; and restricted budgets place limits on subsidized transportation. While many students now have some degree of choice as to which school they will attend, in practice their choices rarely determine the classroom to which they will belong; that decision remains in the hands of school officials.

Choice policies have taken a variety of forms in American education: magnet schools, minischools, alternative schools, vouchers, open enrollment, and post-secondary options for high school students are only some of the most publicized versions of choice. All of these policies present students with a menu of schools from which to select, according to their preferences. Some participants in the choice process have strong preferences and act on them: in the 1980s, some parents in Prince Georges County, Maryland, camped out for days to get a place at the head of the line to sign up for their preferred magnet school. For those who got their preferred choice, the reward was enrollment in a school with a particular curriculum, principal, group of teachers, and group of fellow students that included many who had chosen (or whose families had chosen for them) to attend that school. When students and families are so strongly committed to their choices, they are likely to come to school with a great deal of energy and desire to succeed. That energy and sense of shared commitment are likely to make their school's classrooms more productive than they would be otherwise, some have argued.

Still, the menu of schools from which students and families choose does not tell them the classroom to which they will be assigned or who their classmates or teacher will be, even under the most radical choice policies. This absence of classroom choice suggests that most school-choice plans are likely to have mixed and inconsistent results, simply because students and teachers can easily wind up in classrooms for which they are poorly suited.

Current school-choice plans have not dealt explicitly with the key questions about classrooms: How much do classrooms vary within schools of choice? What happens to students and teachers assigned to classrooms that they find unsatisfactory within the school they have chosen? Is there a conflict between a school's need to advertise a uniform and consistent instructional package, in order to attract students, and the unavoidable realities of classroom differences? And if classrooms in a school vary a great deal in the methods they use and the quality of the education they provide (as they presumably will), how can students and their parents rationally choose a school? These questions underline the fact that teaching and learning take place in individual classrooms that inevitably will differ greatly, even within a given school. Choosing a school without being able to choose one's classroom means that teachers and students cannot know what their daily experiences will be like, or how they will be treated. School-choice policies thus may have only a modest chance to alter classroom membership in ways that will improve students' education. Presumably, as choice plans receive more public examination, proponents will turn their attention to the classroom-membership issues in their proposals.

Even if school-choice policies do not directly address classroom-membership issues, they may still influence education in classrooms—but not because of economic competition between schools, their proponents' favorite incentive. School-choice policies perhaps can best be understood as an elaborate means of *recruiting* teachers and students to a particular school. Alternative schools and minischools recruit teachers by offering them the chance to work with a curriculum and colleagues of their own choosing; students are attracted for the same reason. Choice policies achieve their effects in the same ways as recruiting policies: when school-choice policies attract and retain teachers and students in schools—thereby reducing the normal turnover in student enrollments and faculty—they contribute to the improved functioning of classrooms. When school-choice policies force school officials to be responsive to the requests of teachers, students, and parents for support for their classrooms, choice policies are likely to recruit plenty of teachers and students. In a choice scheme, if a school suffers a decline in applications from new students and teachers, that signal can create pressure on officials to intervene in troubled classrooms in that school (as well as increase efforts to recruit skilled teachers and support them and their classrooms once they arrive).

All of these possible benefits of school-choice policies in actuality are due to an increased emphasis on recruitment. School choice is less a matter of economic competition than it is of marketing, that is, attracting teachers and students to schools where they will be allowed to build their own classrooms. Perhaps school-choice policies could do even more to improve teaching and learning if they also encouraged *classroom* choices (in chapter 8, that possibility will be examined in detail).

The four major classroom-membership policies—classroom assignments, attendance, recruiting, and classroom choice—all grow out of the recognition that to be effective, education policies must build on teachers' and students' self-selection decisions. They do this in several ways: they use the information and preferences of teachers and students to match them to classrooms where they can work productively; they attack the causes of teachers' and students' decisions not to attend school regularly, and to move from one school to another in mid-year; they put pressure on school officials to provide assistance to troubled classrooms, so that dissatisfied teachers and students will not leave for better opportunities elsewhere; they offer tangible benefits—increased teacher salaries, improved working conditions, school programs tailored to student interests—to draw energetic teachers and students to inner-city schools; they use the strong policy of moving students and teachers to new classrooms when they perform poorly; they stimulate teachers and students to work harder by rewarding them with the gift of "being chosen" for a desirable school. In all of these examples, teachers' and students' self-selection decisions stimulate them to work out their own methods of improving student achievement, while taking advantage of the differences among classrooms. They are quintessentially pluralistic policies, imposing no prescriptions on classrooms. Putting the policies into practice will be challenging and not without difficulties; but currently, they are largely kept off the policy agenda by the partisans of the stagnant, familiar policy debate.

Classroom Support Policies

Perhaps even more challenging than designing classroom-membership policies is the problem of finding policies whose effectiveness grows out of classroom reciprocal power. Obviously, such policies must take different forms in each classroom, which is one reason why they don't fit the conventional mold of prescriptive education policies. The goal of class-room-oriented policies is to discover ways to support people in each classroom as they pursue whatever methods of teaching and learning are effective for them, while pressing them to do less of whatever prevents them from teaching and learning. The goal of these classroom-support policies is to improve student achievement, while taking advantage of the central role of reciprocal power in tailoring each classroom's activities to its members.

The school officials who have the greatest opportunity to carry out policies that are built on classroom reciprocal power are principals. Their knowledge of the teachers and students in their schools allows them to design precise, appropriate responses to classroom problems. Most education policy makers expect principals to proclaim and enforce uniform, centrally designed policies in their schools. However, principals are likely to be far more successful if they respond to and provide support for the varied work styles of people in classrooms. Many principals are aware of this; the classroom-support policies discussed here are built on the ideas and work of those principals.[18]

The fact that every classroom is different, even within the same school, means that principals (and other policy makers) need the flexibility to respond to these differences. Their support for teaching and learning must be ad hoc—that is, attending to specific problems as they arise in individual classrooms. The dictionary defines ad hoc as meaning "for this specific purpose; for this use only." In schools, one might add, "for this classroom only." The passion for uniformity of top decision makers in education has given ad hoc measures an undeservedly bad reputation. Ad hoc policies can be as simple as changing the classroom assignment of a student

who seems to be beyond the reach of his or her teacher—
to give both student and teacher a chance to try again, with
different arrangements of classroom reciprocal power. When
the principal waives school rules that prevent people in a
classroom from solving a problem in a novel way, ad hoc
policy making is being used. The fact that every classroom
develops its own distinctive working relationships and solutions to problems is an opening for ad hoc policy making—
for policies of toleration if work is going well, for policies of
intervention if it goes badly. A well-informed principal who
follows this approach will tolerate a classroom's deviation
from official school policies when its students are learning,
and will intervene when they are not. The intervention, if
called for, also will be ad hoc, combining suggestions for
classroom improvements, assistance for the teacher, and reassignments of students poorly matched to that classroom. The
teacher can also be offered an opportunity to work with an
instructional specialist selected by the teacher.

In order for school policies to support classrooms, officials
must know what kind of support is needed; they must become
experts on their classrooms. Many school principals have always paid attention to their teachers' wishes and requests in
order to encourage them, keep them from leaving, and help
them respond to their students' idiosyncratic learning problems. Ad hoc official policies toward teachers can be combined with broader policies of classroom support, such as
creating curriculum libraries and test-item banks, so that
teachers can get new ideas for refining their lessons, adapting
them to their students' needs and strengths, and providing
interesting and challenging tests that encourage students to
think. In addition, policy makers should promote flexibility
in classrooms: there is evidence that when teachers and students are encouraged to adapt instructional approaches to fit

their own classrooms, student achievement improves.[19] Fortunately, the many school principals who listen, observe, and work out classroom-by-classroom solutions to problems are already discreetly practicing the lessons of ad hoc classroom policies.

When classroom reciprocal power produces undesirable results—for example, agreements among people in a classroom to avoid conflict by avoiding the work of teaching and learning[20]—principals can use ad hoc policies to press teachers and students to get on with their work. Sometimes this requires the principal's intervention in classroom discipline, the reassignment of one or two students, or just close, sustained observation of the classroom by the principal.[21] Sometimes even more drastic measures are necessary, depending on the reasons for a particular classroom's failure. The point of targeting interventions on individual classrooms is to protect the efforts of members who want to teach and learn, while avoiding painting other classrooms with the same broad brush that inevitably will be inappropriate for most of them.

Another way for policy makers to take advantage of the diversity among classrooms created by students' and teachers' reciprocal power is to design classroom-improvement strategies that are highly adaptable, flexible, and open to the choices of people in classrooms. The psychiatrist James Comer has worked to improve low-achieving inner-city schools by showing teachers ways to help primary-grade students learn to behave well in school, and helping parents become involved in their children's education.[22] In the first school Comer studied in depth, his team of mental health specialists and child development experts met frequently with the school's teachers. The teachers' problems and questions provided the agenda for these meetings, and the experts provided suggestions that were explicitly adapted to the teachers' particular classroom situations. School policies were changed so that teachers stayed with students for two years, to increase the stability of classroom membership. As new outreach activities led parents to trust the school, they helped their children to attend more regularly. Teachers learned how to respond to students' behavior problems while reducing their use of punishments, and their confidence in their ability to help their students greatly increased. The response from the students was a dramatic improvement in attendance, and a gradual but impressive improvement in achievement, as well. Comer never told teachers how to run their classrooms; he provided ideas and support that could be adapted to the idiosyncrasies of each classroom.

Another pluralistic policy that takes account of classroom reciprocal power is to provide competitive minigrants for teachers.[23] In school districts that follow this approach, teachers can apply for awards of approximately fifty to a few hundred dollars, to pay the costs of implementing their ideas for improving their classroom's work. The grants provide an incentive for teachers and students to develop their own solutions to classroom problems. The minigrant policy sends the message that improvements in teaching and learning will be rewarded. The fact that grants are used differently in each classroom reinforces the idea that teaching and learning can succeed in a wide variety of ways.

The availability of support from surrounding classrooms is another way of fostering classroom improvements. Milbrey McLaughlin's and Dale Mann's research on innovative school programs found that when a "critical mass" of classrooms in a single school was simultaneously involved in a new program, the new program was much more likely to succeed than if it was carried out by a single classroom in each school, working in isolation.[24] One reason for the impact of this critical mass of classrooms is that people in collaborating classrooms can clearly see that their *future* classmates and teachers also are committed to the school's new program. The result is greater acceptance of the new program by teachers and students.

Other examples of policies that support classrooms while adapting to classroom differences involve changing the school's daily schedule—by lengthening high school classes from one to two hours, or giving a school's faculty the flexibility to design some other schedule, or supporting primary-grade teachers' flexible use of class time. Extra-long "block classes" can intensify and sustain the high school classroom's working relationships, without dictating how teaching and learning will be carried out.* The common insight of mini-grants, critical mass classroom changes, and schedule changes is to help people in each classroom do more of whatever teaching and learning practices are effective for them.

All of these classroom-support policies strengthen teachers' and students' own efforts to make their classrooms work, rather than trying to make their behavior conform to a rigid prescription. Clearly, classroom-support policies are pluralistic. They also are designed to be robust: to be changed according to the choices of teachers and students, while still being educationally useful. Another critical difference between classroom-support policies and conventional approaches to improving education is that these policies make use of the detailed knowledge teachers and students have about their classrooms and about each other. Teachers' and students' daily experiences provide them with an abundance of information about the people, events, and unfolding his-

---

*"Block classes" were observed by the author at the High School in the Community, in New Haven, Connecticut, where they have been in use for twenty years.

tory of their classrooms. This is *usable* knowledge,[25] knowledge that points to new opportunities for improving teaching and learning, to new solutions to classroom problems, and to new uses of the classroom's own resources to solve its problems. None of this detailed knowledge about individual classrooms is available to policy makers. Consequently, information about classroom differences is ignored in the policy debate. It is, however, information that teachers and students can use, if given the chance, to improve teaching and learning in their classrooms.

Improving Existing Policies

Policies that have grown out of the education policy debate are overwhelmingly prescriptive; their great weakness is that they take no account of differences among classrooms. Yet there may be opportunities to improve some prescriptive policies by considering the implications of classroom differences, implications that loom large for such issues as the bilingualism-immersion debate, Chapter 1 programs, and school-based management.

For each of these topics, the crucial lesson is that prescriptive policies can only succeed if they are changed so that they adapt to the strengths and needs of individual classrooms. Because I am far from being an expert on the policies discussed in this section, I leave the hard work of gathering the relevant classroom information and technical knowledge needed to apply this lesson to those with the most direct involvement and experience in these policy issues: the teachers, parents, and program specialists concerned with the needs of the children affected by the policies.

Bilingualism and English immersion. The problem of how to educate students whose English abilities are limited has long plagued American schools. Currently, two well-entrenched camps struggle over how to serve non-English-speaking students. On one side are bilingual educators, who favor providing education that is partly conducted in students' native tongue and partly in English, until the student is ready to function well in an all-English classroom. On the other side are educators who favor immersing children in an all-English school environment, to stimulate mastery of English as soon as possible. Research on the effects of these two approaches is hotly disputed.

Both camps advocate prescriptive policies: one prescribes bilingualism, while the other prescribes English immersion. A severe problem confronts both: requiring that teachers and students follow whichever prescription has been endorsed in their community seems tantamount to guaranteeing failure for all classrooms that do not adapt successfully to that prescription. The highly prescriptive nature of these strategies makes it overwhelmingly likely that they will be inappropriate for many classrooms.

The often-repeated result of past evaluations probably will recur in the bilingualism-immersion fight: both approaches are likely to be found to succeed in a few classrooms, fail in a few classrooms, and have mixed effects or none in most classrooms—which would account for the confusing and contradictory findings of bilingual and immersion studies.

Both bilingual and immersion policies can be greatly improved if they take advantage of information possessed by teachers, students, and parents. They know which approach is best suited to their needs, and which suits their experience.[26] Teachers know what kind of training and assistance they will need to deal with students with limited English proficiency, whether they use the bilingual or the immersion approach. Discussing with teachers, students, and parents their ideas and preferences will provide policy makers with crucial information that is currently excluded from the debate. Additional information can come from principals, who can judge whether a particular classroom's problems with attendance or student achievement indicate the need for an adjustment in its language-related instructional methods.

Since it is students and teachers who in the end will do the work of making bilingual or immersion classrooms effective, their information should be weighed heavily in decisions on classroom membership and classroom support. Both approaches may be quite successful in some classrooms; the problem for school officials is to determine which classrooms can do the job with which methods. Given the consistent findings of the policy-implementation studies, it is probable that most classrooms will adapt and alter the bilingual prescription *and* the immersion prescription. Helping classrooms do so in ways that are educationally successful may be the real challenge facing educators of children with limited English proficiency.

Ad hoc implementation is a particularly valuable approach for bilingual and immersion programs, because it allows participants in individual classrooms to determine through experience how well they are doing, what program adjustments they need to make in their classrooms, what additional support they need, and importantly, whether some students and teachers would be better suited to a different kind of classroom. Following this logic, it may be useful for school districts to support classrooms' adaptations of *both* bilingual and immersion methods, rather than prescribing one or the other as the single approved method of instruction. For policy makers, the clear lesson of past policies is that successful classrooms are those that develop their own hybrid approaches, combining methods that work best for their particular teacher and students.

Chapter 1.　As the largest program designed to benefit disadvantaged children, Chapter 1 (which takes its name from the section of the federal legislation that authorizes it) reimburses local school districts for the costs of providing special services to poor, low-achieving students. Historically, Chapter 1 funds have been spent to pay the salaries of specialized teachers who provide remedial instruction to eligible students. Often this instruction takes place in "pull-out" classes—participating students are pulled out of their classroom to spend an hour working with the Chapter 1 teacher. As was argued earlier, the result of this method is that the regular classroom proceeds with its work while the Chapter 1 students are out, often causing them to fall even further behind.

Chapter 1 is a prescriptive program, although unintentionally so. The need to account accurately for federal funds has led local school districts to spend money on easily identifiable, audit-proof services, and the easiest way to do this is with pull-out classes. There are, however, less prescriptive alternatives. For example, Chapter 1 funds could be divided among the teachers of eligible students, who could use them to purchase services to help solve specific classroom problems. Current specialized staff would essentially become consultants, marketing their services to Chapter 1 classrooms, and thus would possess strong incentives to make themselves valuable to the Chapter 1 teachers and students.[27] Teachers might, for example, choose to purchase consultants' technical assistance on ways to meet the needs of particular Chapter 1 students in their classrooms. This approach is similar to

James Comer's use of mental health consultants, who answered teachers' questions and provided training that was tailored to solving specific problems in their classrooms.[28]

Classroom teachers (and parents, too) could band together to use Chapter 1 funds in more creative ways: they might use some funds to support home visits by classroom teachers and Chapter 1 specialists; they might use the funds to support team teaching; they might work with colleagues to discuss better ways to match low-achieving students to classrooms in which they can learn most effectively. All of these examples point to ways in which Chapter 1 could be tailored to individual classrooms. The applications of classroom-oriented approaches to Chapter 1 are limited only by the ideas of the people in those classrooms. Chapter 1 programs currently are not well adapted to the different classrooms it aims to serve. The most attractive option for reaching this goal is to shift Chapter 1 resources from centralized school district control to the classrooms where Chapter 1 students are taught. Finding ways to tailor this huge program to individual classrooms is its greatest challenge.

Chapter 1 is most important in the inner-city schools where large numbers of poor and low-achieving students live. It would be foolish to pretend that there are simple recipes that can solve the problems faced by these schools. Their problems are so grave that it will take more than Chapter 1 funds to fix them. However, local school districts' need for audit information has driven Chapter 1 to become a prescriptive program that treats all affected classrooms alike—and, therefore, treats them all badly. Breaking that cycle, and in particular, finding ways to match low-achieving students with teachers and classrooms that can help them succeed, would be an important way for Chapter 1 to contribute to solving the problems in inner-city schools. Thus, Chapter 1 could be used to support the work by teachers and parents that is needed to change individual classrooms and the ways that students are assigned to them.

School-based management.   Partly as a result of the effective schools movement, and partly in response to strong criticisms of bureaucratic control of the schools, much attention has been given recently to proposals for school-based management. There is little agreement on what this term means. Some of the reforms carried out under its banner include increasing the authority of principals, decentralizing budgets so that schools are permitted to spend a limited amount of money without prior central office approval, and turning the responsibility for governing schools over to groups made up of teachers, parents, and the principal.

These approaches are likely to succeed or fail based on the quality of decisions made by individual school-management teams, and it is safe to predict that the quality of those decisions will vary enormously. However, there are two issues not fully addressed by proponents of school-based management that will surely affect the success of these plans. The first is whether there will be pressure on school-based management teams to produce specified results quickly. The greater the pressure, the more tempting it will be for school teams to rely on the familiar crutch of prescriptive policies, rather than on untested nonprescriptive policies. In the variants of school-based management that place great pressure on the principal to produce results quickly, his or her inclinations to be prescriptive or to take the risk of accepting classroom differences will be crucial, as will his or her willingness to use new classroom-membership and classroom-support policies despite the need for quick results. Sadly, short-term accountability may turn out to be the enemy of needed innovations.

The second (and related) issue is whether school-management teams will pay attention to classroom differences. If they do, they will have an opportunity to apply powerful classroom-membership and classroom-support policies; if they do not, they are unlikely even to consider such policies. In schools where teachers are part of the management team, their willingness to discuss classroom differences and needs (about which they may be acutely sensitive) will determine their ability to devise effective policies. Only when school-based management teams confront classroom differences will they make progress toward solving classroom problems.

School-based management is an empty vessel, waiting to be filled with specific proposals adapted to particular schools and to particular classrooms. Whether it becomes another vehicle for prescriptive policies, or stimulates school people to invent new ways to meet the needs of individual classrooms, is yet to be seen.

What is most important in these three examples is not the specific policy suggestions, but more general themes: that classroom differences matter; that policies can succeed only when adapted to the needs of particular classrooms; that teachers, students, parents, and principals have information about classrooms crucial to any policy's success, but not available to policy makers. The power of policies that are based on these themes stems from a simple truth: they take classrooms seriously.

The Newton Solution:
What Parents and Teachers Can Do Now

EDUCATION policy research has largely confined itself to writing prescriptions for politicians and school officials; it offers virtually no advice for parents and teachers, except to wait, patiently and quietly, for school officials to take action. Because the experts believe that improving education requires changes in curricula, testing, teacher training, remedial classes, and school management, they have no way to speak to the immediate, day-to-day concerns and needs of parents and teachers.

Improving the quality of public schools will require major policy changes, such as those described in the previous chapter, that take account of the central role of the classroom in education. This chapter describes what parents and teachers can do in the meantime. It focuses on the strongest and most direct action that parents and teachers can take to affect a student's educational experience: changing the student's classroom assignment. The power of this approach is supported by the abundant evidence showing that a student's learning gains depend on the classroom to which he or she belongs. This action must be taken with great care, however, because its results are difficult to predict.

Many readers, including education policy makers, will be surprised to learn that this approach has already been accepted and put into practice in a few leading American school districts. I call it the Newton Solution, from the name of the school district where I first learned of it. Newton, Massachusetts is a large and prosperous suburb of Boston. Its families are relatively affluent, and include many professionals and two-earner households. Their involvement in Boston's academic, high-tech, medical, and financial sectors means that Newton's residents do not need to be persuaded of the importance of education in their children's lives; education is a kind of secular religion in Newton. The Newton public schools are relatively well funded, have a history of recruiting and retaining skilled and experienced teachers, and are believed by many observers to be among the best in the nation. But the Newton schools are by no means avant-garde; their reputation is built on solid, American-suburban-style schooling.

I was therefore startled to discover, as I listened to the conversation of a group of Newton parents several years ago, that they were already acting on the ideas about classroom membership that this book presents. The parents were discussing a matter of the utmost importance to them: their children's classroom assignments for the following school year. With great gusto, they exchanged information about the teachers, classmates, and classrooms to which their children might be assigned. There was no evidence of dissatisfaction with any of the teachers whose classes were being discussed; indeed, there seemed to be agreement that all of the teachers were thoughtful and skilled. Yet these parents were preparing themselves to ask the principal of their children's school for particular classroom assignments. Their reasons varied, but came down to one overarching concern: they were seeking the best possible fit between their child, a teacher, and a group of classmates. That is the Newton Solution.

One parent argued that her son needed more structure than one of the teachers in the next grade would provide, while another, who agreed that the teacher in question used an informal and spontaneous classroom style, thought that her daughter would flourish in that classroom. Another hot topic was the issue of potential classmates—the mix of boys and girls, extroverts and introverts, the loud and the silent, the teasers and the teased. One parent said that she would willingly accept any classroom assignment for her son, as long as it separated him from two children in his previous classroom who she believed had distracted him from schoolwork. While I have no way of determining the accuracy or inaccuracy of these parents' characterizations of the teachers and children they discussed, it was clear to me that they were trying to get the best information they could before requesting particular classroom assignments for their children.

When I asked them whether they expected the principal to listen to their requests, I discovered that they—like many other Newton parents—were no novices in the business of influencing their children's classroom memberships. They had started doing it when their children first enrolled in school. And they had found that in Newton, principals listen: according to the parents I spoke with, persistent parents usually get what they request.

The Newton parents are not alone. Across the continent, in Berkeley, California, a similar process has become part of the basic functioning of the public school system. Each year in the spring, parents of elementary school children in Berkeley are asked which teacher they want their child assigned to in the next school year, and principals try to accommodate the parents' requests, within the constraints of class size and ethnic balance.

What is going on in Newton and Berkeley, and in all the other communities that use the Newton Solution, is an institutionalized process of involving parents (and teachers) in the classroom assignment process in an effort to produce the best possible educational experiences for students. The Newton Solution is based on three facts:

1. Every classroom is different from other classrooms, even those in the same school; the differences are caused by the particular teacher and students who are members of each classroom.
2. Classroom differences are a crucial determinant of students' learning.
3. Detailed information on individual teachers, students, and classrooms—information that is highly relevant to classroom assignment decisions—is possessed by parents and teachers, not just by principals and guidance counselors.

Taken together, these propositions point to the reasons for the Newton Solution: parents and teachers have information that is vital to classroom assignment decisions, and it makes sense for them to use this information to help shape the membership of new classrooms.

The Newton Solution also underscores the importance of this book's central argument: schools are not homogeneous; they are made up of a diverse collection of classrooms in which teaching and learning take place in a wide variety of ways. Even troubled schools have classrooms that may be able to serve many students well, if students are assigned to particular classrooms where they can work effectively. All of the education reform movements have been built on the assumption that when students in a school are not learning, the whole school (and its curriculum, teachers, instructional methods, and management) needs to be reformed. This focus on the school as a whole misses the central fact on which the Newton Solution is based: schools don't educate students, classrooms do—and classrooms in a school differ from each other. Smart parents pay attention to *classrooms.*

The Newton Solution requires no action from the Education President, Congress, state legislatures, or voters. It can be put into practice by parents, teachers, and principals. Its goal is to get each student, and especially each low-achieving student, into the classroom where he or she can learn the most and work most effectively; and if the first attempt to do that fails, to move that student to another classroom that can do the job better.

How It Works

By drawing on twenty years of experience in Newton, Berkeley, and elsewhere across the country, it is possible to see how a school's classroom assignment process can make use of the information possessed by parents and teachers. In most cases, the school principal sends a letter to all parents in the spring of the year, inviting them to write a letter describing the kind of classroom, teacher, and classmates to which they would prefer to have their child assigned. Sometimes parents are invited to request a particular teacher or particular classmates.* The principal's letter may explain the reasons that not every request can be accommodated—for example, because the full roster of teachers for the following year is not yet known. Principals who discourage requests for particular teachers may accept other kinds of requests—for open or traditional classrooms, strong or flexible discipline, and so forth. The letters are used along with suggestions from the students' current teachers to devise classroom assignment lists. Parents are then informed of their children's assignments by June. In Newton and Berkeley, these practices are now completely accepted, having gradually evolved from earlier, informal negotiations between parents and school staff regarding students' classroom assignments.

Roland Barth, a former Newton principal (and now the director of the Principals' Center at Harvard University) used the following text in his annual spring letter to parents:

> The faculty, you, and I all feel that the placement of children in classes for next year is a decision of great importance— one that affects your child's life at Angier [School] for ten months.

> (1) If you have information about your child and about the kind of learning environment in which he best works and learns which would help us in the placement decision, we want you to share this with us by writing me a note before May 16th [two weeks after Barth's letter]. (2) Shortly after all the [parent-teacher] conferences for a grade level have been concluded, the teachers at your child's present grade level, special services (e.g., psychologist, learning disabilities

---

*In some Newton schools, all of the students in a particular grade have the same teachers (one teacher for reading and history, one for math and science, and so forth). In at least one such school, the principal invited parents to indicate which classmates would contribute most to their child's education.

teachers . . .), and I will meet, compile, and discuss all the information we have about your child, and make assignments. (3) We will then inform you in writing of these decisions. If you have questions about the rationale for the decision, comments, or concerns, I would like you to call me or come and see me within a week . . .

In order to maximize children's learning it is essential that equitable, compatible, balanced classes be assembled which reflect what teachers know about the conditions under which your child best functions. You can be sure that throughout the placement process two concerns will be foremost in our minds—that your child will be in a classroom in which he will flourish academically and socially, and that your child will be in a classroom in which you can have confidence.[1]

Barth's letter accurately reflects many principals' belief that while parents have important information about their children that is relevant to classroom assignments, and while as parents and taxpayers they have a right to have their requests treated seriously, other factors should also be given weight in the classroom assignment process. His letter does make it clear, however, that parents are invited to make requests and to add their information to the classroom assignment process.

In the years Barth sent his letter to parents, they responded eagerly: up to 60 percent wrote back. These high levels of parent involvement are not wholly the product of Barth's solicitation of letters; he reports that even before he asked for it directly, parental input "had been going on for a long time, but under the table. Lots of informal arrangements were made [with teachers and principals], but just with 10 percent or so of the parents. What was new was inviting them in."[2] It seems likely that in Newton and elsewhere, many parents have been using the Newton Solution for a long time, whether or not they received invitations from their school's principal to take part in the classroom assignment process.

While he believes that parents should request but not dictate classroom assignments, Barth records in his book *Run School Run* the fact that in his school, parents who were dissatisfied with their child's initial classroom assignment decision, and who persisted in their requests for a different assignment, usually got what they wanted. He writes, "If after the conferences, the phone calls, the letters, and the hallway discussion parents still demand a change, I usually give in. . . . Generally, we think it makes sense to accede to parents' demands if they are very strong. If we don't change the child's teacher, everyone will be miserable [due to parents' communicating their displeasure to their child]. If we do make the change, the worst that can happen is that the child will not have the best possible year. It seems a reasonable trade."[3]

Currently all of the schools in Newton encourage parents to make their classroom assignment preferences known to principals. The district's policy is that each principal is responsible for classroom assignment decisions in his or her building, and that parent concerns are to be taken into account. According to Newton officials, having principals explicitly seek parents' views "eliminates the feeling among parents [that the only way to get their preferred assignment is to] . . . be aggressive and strong-arm the principal."[4]

In Berkeley, all primary and elementary schools (kindergarten through sixth grade) send a letter to parents each spring listing the teachers who will be teaching their child's grade in the following school year. Parents are asked to indicate their preference for their child's classroom teacher. The letters typically ask parents to list more than one preference. Parents whose children will be starting kindergarten are also invited to make their preferences known. School officials tell parents that their preferences will be treated seriously, but cannot be guaranteed by the school, because of the need to balance classes' size, ethnic makeup and other factors. The schools try to make sure that parents who do not receive their first preference in a given year will do so the following year.[5]

High school students in Berkeley make their own classroom selections in a process called self-scheduling, which resembles registration at a large university. After meeting with a guidance counselor who tells them which courses they are required to take and offers course suggestions, students submit a list of the courses they plan to take, and school officials tally the lists to create a master schedule of all the classes that will be offered. Then the self-scheduling takes place: tables are set up in the gym, with one table offering a choice of all of the English classes, and others offering the math classes, the history classes, and so on. Students get in line at the tables offering the courses that they want. When a student reaches the head of the line, he or she selects a class section (that is, a teacher, course, and meeting time) from those that have space available.[6] Students can thus select their courses, teachers, and even classmates (by conferring with other students and making their choices together).

In what may be the only comparative study of classroom assignment practices, Cornell's David Monk conducted a survey of seventeen elementary schools serving varied socioeconomic classes in five states. He found that principals reported receiving classroom assignment requests from 1 to 6 percent of parents. Most of the principals either discouraged or did not invite parents to express their classroom preferences. However, all of the principals "seemed genuinely interested in being responsive to parent requests made prior to assignment. . . . The basic view was that satisfied parents provide more support and that this helps the child."[7] Monk found that parents who made early requests and parents who were persistent were likely to have their requests granted. What is fascinating in Monk's findings is their corroboration of the Newton and Berkeley patterns: principals are willing to accept parent requests, provided they can be balanced with other factors; persistence pays off for parents; and parents' information about their children is taken seriously by the schools. This is good news for parents who do not happen to live in Berkeley or Newton; they can still use their own, private version of the Newton Solution.

Two important lessons emerge from Newton, Berkeley, and the other places where parents have become involved in the classroom assignment process. One is that the belief held by some school officials that it is not feasible to permit parents to have a say in their children's classroom assignments is simply false. Twenty years of experience in Newton, Berkeley, and elsewhere proves that parents *can* become involved in classroom assignment decisions without disrupting school operations.

The second lesson is that even without being invited into the process, parents who have strongly held concerns about their child's school success can take an active role in making the single most important decision affecting the child's schooling: the classroom in which he or she will spend the next year. Long before principals in Newton and Berkeley started asking parents about their preferences for their children's classroom assignments, parents were already telling school people what classroom would work best for their child, and why. Indeed, it was the actions of parents, not education policy makers' initiatives, that initially opened up the classroom assignment process in Newton and Berkeley to parental input. Thus, it is clear that parents can take action to influence their child's classroom assignment; the proof is that this is already happening, through informal contacts and formalized processes between parents and school people throughout the country.

What Parents Should Do

When deciding whether they want to become involved in the classroom assignment process, parents should bear in mind several caveats. Even the best teachers may not consistently have successful classrooms, because the teacher is not the sole determinant of classroom success; classmates and unpredictable events strongly shape a classroom's outcomes too. Parents' preferences are sometimes based on superficial knowledge (such as the noise level during a brief visit to a classroom, or inaccurate hearsay about a teacher's reputation), or on factors that apply to the parent but not the child (such as the parent's preference for a highly structured classroom, when an open classroom would be more suitable for the child).[8] Finally, parents may not want or need to become deeply involved in the classroom assignment process, because of their confidence that the school's process takes account of their child's needs. These are all good reasons for parents to hesitate before rushing to involve themselves in the classroom assignment process: they may lack the information, objectivity, or desire to contribute usefully to that process.

At the same time, many parents have valuable information about their child that the schools lack, and may have reason to be dissatisfied with the school's past classroom assignment decisions. They should gather all their information about their child and the classes that are being formed for the next year, and then present the information to the school.

When parents have information about the conditions under which their child is likely to work and learn most effectively during the next school year—including information on their child, as well as on potential teachers, classmates, and kinds of classroom instruction—they should seriously consider becoming involved in the classroom assignment process. This involvement can take the form of writing to the principal, meeting with the child's current teacher, telephoning a formal request to the principal, and following up on these initial actions if the school's response is not satisfactory. By taking these actions, parents will be creating their own version of the Newton Solution.

The best way for parents to apply the Newton Solution will vary from one school to another. Here are some ideas that parents may find helpful in getting the best possible result from the classroom assignment process.

- Call or visit your child's school early in the spring to find out when the classroom assignment decisions for the next school year will be made. It is very important for parents to act *before* the classroom assignments are made.
- Get all the information that you can from the school *and from other parents,* including information about teachers and classrooms in the next grade and information about the children who are your child's potential classmates. Visit and observe your child's current classroom and the classrooms of other teachers in the same and the next grade.
- Be concrete about why your child will work and learn more effectively in one classroom than another.* Give details

---

*David Monk's interviews revealed that principals were willing to listen to factual criticisms of a specific teacher's competence, but strongly rejected comments on teachers' professionalism or integrity.[9]

about your child's particular situation. For example, a child might have one of the following characteristics:

a need for structure, discipline, and being pushed to work, or for a less structured, open instructional approach;

a need to be separated from a twin, a sibling, or a troublesome classmate (if a classmate is a major problem, this may be a more important request than one for a specific teacher);

a need to be with the same teacher for two years, to provide a sense of stability and trust (for example, due to a recent parental divorce);

a need to be in a class with two grades, or one grade, or with physically larger kids, or physically smaller kids, or classmates who are older, and so on, due to the child's developmental stage;

a need for a teacher with a particular personality (nurturing, firm, adventurous, motherly, fatherly, demanding, gentle, well-organized, patient, strict, and so forth);[10]

comments about "specific teacher characteristics and how they affected or would affect a particular child."[11]

- Back up your reasons with specific information about your child and your family situation, if relevant: siblings' experiences with particular teachers,* family issues such as a divorce, or a child's need to avoid in-school criticism from an older sibling.

---

*Among the principals surveyed by Monk, there was "a sense that if a *family* had already experienced a weak or otherwise objectionable teacher, they were exempt from experiencing the same teacher a second time."[12]

• If the school's response is truly unsatisfactory and likely to harm the child, *be persistent*. School staff won't tell you that persistence pays off—why should they?—but it does. Use letters, phone calls, and meetings to convince the school authorities that your reasons are valid.

Parents should also listen to the school's response. School staff have information about your child that you lack, just as you have information that they lack. The principal may have excellent reasons for not accepting your request, and it would be potentially detrimental to your child to ignore the school's rationale for an assignment that is different from the one that you requested.

The steps outlined here contain a consistent theme: gather information about your child and the school, and present it calmly and persistently to the people in the school who make the classroom assignment decisions. That, in a nutshell, is how parents can use the Newton Solution.

Why it is needed

Some readers may regard the Newton Solution as an obvious, commonsensical approach that any reasonable parent and school should use. Sadly, there is reason to believe that many schools currently make classroom assignments with little regard for parent requests *or any other information that might improve the match between a student and his or her classroom.* While there is little systematic evidence on this issue, David Monk's interviews with seventeen elementary school principals found that eleven reported making students' classroom assignments *randomly*—they divided students between teachers without using any information about the ability of the people in a classroom to work with each other. A common classroom assignment method, Monk found, was for the principal to divide the students according to their reading levels, and then randomly to assign a high group, a medium group, and a low group to each classroom.[13] Monk's interviews noted, however, that some of the principals who relied on random methods to assign students to classrooms later altered some assignments in response to feedback from teachers and parents.

If students' achievement were unaffected by the classroom to which they are assigned, these practices would presumably not be much of a problem; but we know that students' achievement *is* dramatically influenced by the classroom to which they belong. Moreover, whether parents' requests are heeded or not, parents' involvement in classroom assignment decisions sends the right messages to school officials: that classroom assignments matter, that officials should take action to make every classroom effective and desirable, and that the schools should adapt to meet the needs of the people in classrooms. Those are the reasons that the Newton Solution is vital to the success of the public schools.

Official resistance

Many parents who have become involved in their child's classroom assignments have been welcomed by school principals. Some principals resist parent involvement, however. A school district administrator in a Northeastern city told me,

> You can't cross the line where the public forgets that the teachers and the principals are the professionals, and they've undergone a lot of training and are paid a reasonable amount of money to make educated decisions in the best interests of

those kids. You can't adopt a policy or practices that would encourage the free-for-all: you know, "No, I don't want my kid to have her, no, I want him over here"; that would just be bad practice. It becomes Let's Make a Deal. Probably the principals there [in Newton] don't last real long.

It's interesting for me, for our family, because we have kids in the school system, and my husband's a vice-principal in the school district. There are some cases where you just divorce yourself from this role, and you go in as a parent, and say, look, this is worth it to me to raise the issue.

In schools of the more affluent parents, you'll have that. Oh, sure you do. Absolutely. I know that we do. Oh, without a doubt.

For this administrator, school officials are the experts and parents should not get involved in their decisions—but affluent parents do anyway, and they get what they want; and she herself has occasionally intervened in her children's schooling. Clearly, she and many other school officials find it difficult to balance their desire for parents to stay out of school decisions with their awareness of the importance of classroom assignments.

It is easy to understand school officials' fear that swarms of parents will converge on the schools, clamoring like game show contestants for the prize behind Door Number Three. The associate superintendent of schools in Berkeley said of his district's acceptance of parent requests: "It's quite a juggling act for the principals. Many principals think it's a pain."[14] (As we shall see, one reason for principals to be wary of parent requests is the pressure they create to deal with the difficult problem of ineffective teachers.) A school superintendent explained why his district does not encourage parents to become part of the classroom assignment process:

> Because it's easier not to do it . . . It really happens now. Perhaps not as a broadcast, overt, organizationally encouraged activity; but it happens right now . . . It's probably a good thing to do. But it's not critical to the operation of the district. At this point. It may become so in the future. So, you know, you deal with one thing at a time, I guess.

"It really happens now": even without being invited to do so, some parents request classroom assignment changes for their children. But "it's easier not to do it": by not publicizing the fact that they do accept parents' requests, school officials minimize the number of requests that they receive. School officials understandably cling to the few things they can control—and classroom assignments are one of those things.

If schools respond to the classroom requests of middle-class parents but close their doors to the requests of less affluent parents, something will have gone badly wrong with our nation—something that *all* parents should try to fix. Spreading the classroom assignment practices of Newton and Berkeley to Boston and Oakland might result in greater educational gains than all of the new curricula and testing programs that are currently at the center of the education policy debate. Perhaps some poor parents will make less informed classroom choices than affluent parents; the following year, their choices will be more informed, and school officials will have gotten better at explaining the school's classroom assignment decisions. Both the parents and the school will benefit from this gradual learning process. The alternative is to tell poor parents, "We know what's best for you and your children. The schools are fine just the way they are. Don't worry, just go quietly to sleep, and leave the schools alone." The record of that approach is too well known to repeat here.

Even if their appeals are rejected, parents stand to gain a

great deal: information about their child's school and classroom, which they can use later on; knowledge about the politics involved in influencing a principal's decision; awareness of the differences between classrooms in their child's school. Schooling takes place over a long period of time; principals change; and parents who remember last year's struggle will have a better chance of winning this year's.

There is a long and deeply rooted history of conflict between parents and school people; their lives are "worlds apart," to use Sara Lawrence Lightfoot's evocative phrase.[15] The price of more parent and student involvement, of course, will be new demands placed on school officials—to respond to information and requests received from parents and students, and to decide what to do about ineffective teachers who are not requested. However, it is important to note that these demands are likely to improve the quality of the schools, by focusing school staff members' energies on improving their school's classrooms.

One of the key issues mentioned by school officials who resist the involvement of parents in classroom assignment decisions is the problem of what to do when a teacher is not chosen by parents. Some principals recognize that one reason that this may happen is that the teacher may simply not be very effective. In these cases, the problem should not be seen as one of parents' reluctance to have their children in that teacher's classroom. Even if the distraught parents vanished overnight, the teacher's performance would still be a problem. The experiences of Newton and Berkeley make it clear that the appropriate response to this problem is the honest one: discussing with the teacher why parents say they are not satisfied, thus turning a disturbing situation into an opportunity for improvement. Roland Barth, the former Newton principal, gave this example:

I recall a class to which neither teachers nor parents wanted to send many children. I sat with the teacher for many hours. . . . [This] provoked much soul-searching and stimulated considerable change the following year. There is much to be said for these kinds of direct, head-on confrontations.[16]

Clifford Wong, the associate superintendent in Berkeley, described his principals' approach: "The teachers with lots of vacancies" [after parents submit their requests] are told what has happened, "to get them to be more responsive to parents' concerns."[17] It does teachers no favor to withhold this information from them, for there may be much that they can do to improve their classrooms. Indeed, the sometimes uncomfortable messages to teachers that result from being watched by parents may make the schools more effective in the long run. Instead of being shrouded in a silence of no pressures for change, schools and teachers will hear anxious, perceptive, concerned voices that they cannot ignore.[18] If they respond to those voices, the children they serve will benefit—as will society at large. School decisions on issues such as teacher hiring and teachers' tenure may also be improved by vigorous parent requests for classrooms where their children can learn.

The most difficult situations are those facing parents whose children's schools include few classrooms in which effective teaching and learning take place. If there are no desirable classrooms, then the Newton Solution can offer no short-term improvements. Loud expressions of parental dissatisfaction will be required to get school officials to improve such schools. Drawing school officials' attention to unsatisfactory classrooms is an excellent way for parents to begin organizing to change their children's schools. The Newton Solution is not a one-shot, one-year, miracle solution: parents can use it every year for as long as their children are in school.

For school officials, the Newton Solution provides a constant push to pay attention to the most important thing in any school: the quality of its classrooms. In some school systems, parental feedback may even serve to trigger the process of removing ineffective teachers and recruiting effective ones. But even if less effective teachers remain, many of them can improve their performance by responding to the messages they get from the Newton Solution, and by using other approaches discussed in this book. (The issues regarding ineffective teachers who do not improve are discussed in detail in chapter 9.)

Mid-year classroom changes

The same evidence that supports parental involvement in the classroom assignment process also suggests that when a student is doing badly in class—particularly if the student's failure represents a change from his or her previous school performance—the strongest response may be to move the student to another classroom.* With another teacher, another set of classmates, and a new collection of reciprocal power relationships shaping the student's behavior, he or she may be able to work more effectively. On the other hand, parents should be aware that the evidence does not rule out the possibility that the new classroom may be no more successful than the original one. Another reason for parents to exercise caution in seeking a mid-year transfer is the evidence that classrooms with high student turnover produce smaller

*On a very different scale, school people intervene in classrooms every day when they send troublesome students to the principal's office, thereby removing them from their classrooms. A mid-year change in a student's classroom assignment can be seen as removing the student from class for the rest of the year, but with a greatly increased opportunity for the student to make educational gains in the new classroom.

achievement gains than other classrooms.[19] However, the disappointing record of remedial education policies, combined with the evidence on classroom achievement differences, means that a change in classroom assignment is likely to have much stronger effects than other changes (constant reteaching, small group remediation, referral to additional services, and so forth). When a student is having a disastrous year in his or her assigned classroom, without any clearly evident and treatable cause, parents should consider asking the school to move the student to another classroom.

This mid-year version of the Newton Solution is less likely to be accepted by school officials than is a parent's classroom request for the following year. Principals are under pressure to keep classroom sizes roughly equal; they are understandably worried about unleashing a torrent of capricious requests from parents for classroom changes; and they are sensitive to the criticism of themselves and their teachers that a request for a different classroom implies.[20] All of these factors make them reluctant to accept parents' requests for a mid-year change of classrooms. However, Monk found that all of the principals he interviewed said that they would agree to a mid-year classroom change "for legitimate reasons or if a parent was unusually insistent. These . . . changes were considered to be unfortunate, and principals viewed themselves as choosing the lesser of two evils by agreeing to change a [student's classroom assignment]."[21]

Even principals who understand the importance of a student's classroom assignment may resist parents' requests for mid-year changes. Roland Barth reports that he set up procedural hurdles to get parents to hesitate before requesting a mid-year change.[22] An urban superintendent I interviewed told me, "We require a couple of conversations with guidance counselors and parents, [before] you get the kid out of the class and put him in another class."

My interviews with teachers turned up some interesting reports about how these mid-year changes work. In general, teachers are more sanguine about such changes than are administrators, but they share administrators' suspicions that parents may not know what is best for their children.

> I think the kids here have pretty much flexibility on [changing their classroom assignments in mid-year]; I don't think the school is hostile to that at all. But they have to figure out that they need to move. That's the key issue. That's why I am so thrilled with my Freshman Study Skills kids asking for help. One of the ways they need to ask for help is, "This teacher and I are going nowhere." One of my kids came up to me yesterday and said to me she was getting her Western Civ changed. That was the right choice for her.

> Not every child fits in this classroom. Maybe the principal would hate to hear me say that, but I don't think this is for everybody. *I* would have been a nut in this classroom. Some kids need to be in some other classroom. I have had kids that teachers really had a hard time with in their classrooms, and they were put in here, and there wasn't any problem. We switch kids around, to make it better for that child. Even during the year. It makes it more humane.

> Now, the bad effect is [parents] overriding academic placements, [which is] very common in the ninth and tenth grades—insisting on an honors placement. And 90 percent of the time, the parental request is honored.

What is perhaps most interesting in teachers' reports about mid-year classroom changes is their perception that these changes can improve results not only for the student who is moved, but for them and their other students as well. As their testimony throughout this book makes clear, teachers are quite aware of the fact that classroom differences have strong effects on students (and on teachers); consequently, they are often willing to accept mid-year transfers that appear likely to help students and teachers work and learn better.

What Teachers Can Do

As the teachers' comments in this chapter make clear, the Newton Solution is not just a solution for parents; it works for teachers, too. In many school systems, teachers are kept out of the classroom assignment process; but in Newton and many other places, they play a central role in it. Teachers possess a great deal of information that can be used to improve the quality and effectiveness of classroom assignments. Here are the words of teachers who have been involved in making classroom assignment decisions, both for the following year and for mid-year classroom changes:

> When we get ready to group the children for the following year, the teachers that have the children now meet with the teachers that will get them next year. First we deal with the very difficult children. And each teacher who has children in that category would say a bit about them, and then they would be placed. Sometimes the second grade teacher will say, well, I could deal with that, and I'll take that child. This way, you know which of those children you'd get along better with, or you'd be able to handle. And if there are children that we might like to have in our rooms, for whatever reason, we are free to say that. Or if there is a child that we, for whatever reason, would rather not have, we are free to say that.

I have occasionally gone and said, I know I can't cut it with that kid, he's been assigned to my class, get him somewhere else, it's better for both of us. I've done that. Kids have done the same thing. "I'm in Mr. X's class, this just isn't going to fly, put me somewhere else."

Yes, we do allow for [classroom changes after the year has begun]; at the end of two weeks, we have a meeting. And at that time we talk about any changes that we would like to make. Just the teachers on the same grade level. Then we are free to say if there's any reason that we think there should be any changes. For whatever reason, there can be changes. One year, beyond the two-week period, it happened; we just had to be very specific [in explaining to the principal] about why this should happen. It's really much easier to have the teachers decide.

These teachers use their knowledge about their own classrooms and the information they receive from other teachers and from parents to make recommendations about students' classroom assignments. The feasibility of this approach for improving teaching and learning is demonstrated by the existence of substantial numbers of schools where it is already practiced—probably considerably more schools than invite parents to participate in the classroom assignment process.[23]

David Monk's interviews with principals strongly suggested that "teachers are more attentive [in the classroom assignment process] to subtle differences among students than are principals."[24] Roland Barth identified another benefit of involving teachers in classroom assignment decisions: "When a teacher has to think about a child's optimal learning style for future [classroom] placement, that consideration often affects the current year's instruction in rewarding and productive ways."[25] When teachers are involved in the classroom assignment process, not only do they contribute valuable information, but their teaching may improve, too.

In schools where teachers are not involved in classroom assignment decisions, they still may be able to inject some of the information they possess into that process. However, since schools vary in their procedures, there is no single prescription for teachers to follow. Here are some ideas for teachers to consider:

- they can write memos to their principal or the school's guidance staff regarding the future placement of their current students;
- they can meet with the other teachers at their grade level or in their department to discuss joint recommendations on students' classroom assignments;
- they can arrange for a grade-level or departmental meeting a few weeks after the school year begins, to discuss reassigning students who might work and learn better in a classroom other than their currently assigned one;
- they can recognize that students who are low achievers or troublesome in their current classroom may not be so if reassigned to another classroom, and can discuss the possibility of a reassignment with the school's guidance staff, principal, the potential receiving teacher, and the student.

Increased involvement of teachers in classroom assignment decisions can be complicated. Some of Monk's principals said that some teachers may seek to avoid dealing with hard-to-teach students by pushing to have them assigned to other teachers' classrooms. Monk also noted "an instance where veteran teachers 'loaded up' a first-year teacher with a disproportionate number of difficult students."[26] But even if teachers are occasionally reluctant to cooperate with their peers, they still possess information that is crucial for the effectiveness of the placement process. In the few cases in which cooperation among teachers fails, teachers can submit lists of students who are likely to work well together, along with specific information on the circumstances in which students have worked well in the past, to an unbiased school official who can match the classroom lists with the following year's teachers.

Other resources

For teachers, the Newton Solution is not the only strategy for improving their educational results. They can also take advantage of their classroom's greatest resource: the current membership of the classroom. Instead of focusing on the deficits and handicaps of students, teachers can find out what each student *can* do, and build on the information. If students can help each other learn, if they learn by dramatizing, or by simulating congressional debates, or by writing, or by discussing, or by analyzing their community's and families' issues and concerns—teachers can use these kinds of discoveries about their classroom to form the basis for their teaching. They can also ask other teachers for classroom support, in the form of new ideas, new solutions to classroom problems, new ways to bend the school's rules to get more classroom work done, and new ways to create a reciprocal power relationship that favors learning.

None of the suggestions in this chapter is a prescription or a recipe for school improvement, for the simple reason that if they are to be effective, each of them must be carried out differently by each parent and teacher. They are, instead, recommendations for ad hoc changes in individual families' and individual classrooms' behavior, based on the recognition that the crucible of education is the classroom.

Much has been written about how parents and teachers can respond to educational problems that are not discussed in this chapter: how to respond when the school calls about a child's behavior problem, how to get into a magnet school, what to do when children watch too much television. There are plenty of sources of good advice on these topics; interested readers should seek them out.[27] I have emphasized the Newton Solution because its potential impact has received little public recognition, and because it offers a powerful opportunity for change that the education system has not yet seized.

CHAPTER 9

Helping the System Fix Itself:
Education Policy
from the Point of View
of Students, Teachers, and Parents

AMERICAN education is already in deep trouble, and it is quite possible that it will deteriorate even further. The education policy debate and most of the education reform movements are engaged in a fruitless search for magic-bullet solutions to education's problems, even when all the evidence shows that no magic bullets exist. While the debate continues, the nation's students are caught in an education system that is sliding from mediocrity into outright failure.

The reason for this sad prognosis is that the education system has no built-in way to correct its problems: there is no mechanism that pushes politicians and education policy makers in the right direction. Human beings are not, in general, fools: when things go badly for them, they usually change what they are doing and pursue a more productive course. In education, that self-corrective mechanism does not function because policy makers have not been able to identify ways to improve the schools.

The problem that blocks education policy makers' efforts to fix the system is, at its core, a problem of understanding. In other policy areas, policy makers understand that individuals' choices and actions are part of the policy process. For example, when policy makers think about the marketplace behavior of buyers and sellers, or individuals' choice of a physician, or the decisions of men and women to marry and start families, they recognize that individuals' actions are crucial determinants of the success of the economy, the health care system, and the welfare of children. In these policy arenas, policy makers have devised nonprescriptive methods to influence individuals' behavior by changing the incentives that they face—for example, by altering the rules on physicians' reimbursements. In contrast, education policy makers have chosen to rely on prescriptive policies because they do not understand the behavior of people in classrooms. As a result, education policies are predestined to fail.

The reasons for the disastrous condition of American schools, the research shows, do not lie in poor textbooks, or in the curriculum, or in teaching methods, or in the failure to adopt merit pay plans. Experience and abundant evidence show that for each of the prescriptive solutions designed to solve the schools' problems, a few schools will improve slightly, a few will decline slightly, and most will stay where they are. In other words, the success of prescriptive policies is determined by how well they are implemented by teachers and students: if they are carried out well, student achievement goes up, and if not, student achievement stays the same or declines. Despite the good intentions of every prescriptive policy, the quality of education is ultimately determined by the ad hoc classroom actions of students and teachers. So long as education policy makers fail to understand the classroom crucible, there is little reason to expect education policies to work.

Politicians and policy makers need to recognize the evidence on the crucial role of classrooms in education, and then to change their current direction. The remainder of this chapter is devoted to a discussion of the changes that are needed to steer a course that will improve the schools.

Learning to Pay Attention to Classrooms

The education system is so large and complex that policy makers badly need a simplified way to look at the schools and their problems. This book has argued that there is a way for policy makers and politicians to understand how education works: by paying attention to the actions of students and teachers in their classrooms. The basic principles of this approach can be summed up as follows:

- Teachers and students are the authors of the work that takes place in classrooms, and they develop different methods of doing their work in each classroom.
- Successful teaching and learning can happen in a wide variety of ways; all of them are dependent on the choices and actions of teachers and students.
- Prescriptive policies that are imposed on classrooms do not work.
- The only way for education policies to improve students' achievement is to affect teachers' and students' work in their classrooms, by altering classroom membership or increasing classroom support.

If policy makers and school officials can learn to focus their attention firmly on classrooms, they will have taken the first step toward figuring out how to correct the problems of the schools. By paying attention to classrooms, they can find out where problems exist, what the problems are, and what classroom changes can solve them.

They can take a second important step by recognizing that each classroom is different from all other classrooms—and that therefore solutions to a classroom's problems have to be tailored to the particular characteristics of that classroom. Classrooms differ in their use of books and materials, time, and instructional techniques; in the kinds of rewards and motivations they offer teachers and students; in the unofficial rules that govern daily classroom life; in the ways that classroom members treat each other and how they expect to be treated in the future; and in the opportunities to learn that they provide. These differences render any uniform, prescriptive school policy irrelevant to most classrooms.

This focus on classroom differences represents a fundamentally new and different way of thinking about how education works, and its implications are profound. When policy makers (or parents, for that matter) recognize the importance of classrooms, they will begin to ask new questions about each proposed policy they consider:

- How will this policy and its effects be altered by the large differences between classrooms?
- How will the policy affect classrooms that differ widely in their reciprocal power relationships and in their teaching and learning methods?

Only policies that respond to the needs of different classrooms should receive official support.

Experimenting with Classrooms

If policy makers can give up their fixation on prescribed curricula and teaching methods for classrooms, they can take advantage of powerful new approaches to school improvement. The following policies offer some initial ways to stimulate teachers and students to teach and learn:

- new classroom membership policies (including improved attendance policies, increased parent and student choice of classrooms, and team teaching);
- new classroom support policies (including ad hoc responses by principals, tailored to individual classrooms' problems);
- alternative schools (which recruit new classroom members from the ranks of teachers and students who do not want to work in traditional schools);
- increased teacher salaries (to enlarge and improve the pool of new and returning teachers);
- stabilized classroom memberships (achieved by providing subsidized transportation for students who move during the school year, so they can continue to attend their original classroom; high school classes of two hours in length, to intensify the teaching and learning that take place there; and classes that retain the same membership for two school years); and
- increased school outreach activities aimed at recruiting dropouts to return to school (perhaps by contracting with community-based organizations that would provide support and tutoring, and would be paid according to the number of students they induced to return and graduate—giving these organizations a strong incentive to become classroom advocates for the students and to encourage them to remain in school).

These proposals strengthen the ability of people in classrooms to teach and learn, while avoiding prescriptions that ignore classroom differences.

Stronger classrooms can solve other problems, as well. For example, considerable evidence points to the transitions from elementary school to junior high, and from junior high to high school, as trigger points for school failure.[1] One explanation for this problem is the reduction in support that students may experience as they switch from an all-day classroom, with a single set of classmates and a single teacher, to constant changes of classes, classmates, and teachers, few of whom they know well. Policies that alter classroom assignments in students' first year in the new school so that they stay with the same group of classmates for most of the day (for their major academic subjects, for example) can use the power of classroom membership to support students as they make this difficult transition. One experiment that used this approach caused a substantial reduction in the incidence of dropping out.[2] Of course, such policies cannot work if students' classrooms are themselves failing; high dropout rates should always signal school officials of the need to focus on the effectiveness of classrooms.

These classroom experiments will require new kinds of policy research. If policy makers really want to determine the effectiveness of education policies, rigorous studies that use an experimental design are the way to do that.* The results of experiments will only be believed if the standards of education policy research are raised so that experimen-

---

*Such studies have been widely used in welfare policy and employment and training policy, where they have proved to be extremely successful. These studies use a control group to measure what happens without the new policy, compared to the performance of the experimental group, who are affected by the policy. Note that random assignment of students (or in some cases, schools) to the experimental and control groups is a required element of these studies.

tal designs become the dominant form of policy research. The fact that ten years after the "effective schools" movement first received national attention, there has been no rigorous experiment determining the impacts of the "effective schools" techniques, demonstrates the limited use that education research makes of the most powerful research methods.

Facing the Issue of the Quality of the Teacher Force

Every parent of a child in the schools today knows of good teachers and ineffective teachers. So do their elected representatives, who regularly receive parents' angry complaints. As a direct result of this situation, there is widespread public and legislative resentment of teachers. Voters wonder why they should spend large sums of money on teachers' salary increases—one of the key elements of a classroom membership policy that will improve the schools—when a significant share of the increases will go to reward current teachers, some of whom are not helping their students learn. Until this public resentment is confronted head on, many state legislatures will not vote for the salary increases that are necessary.

It is important to recognize that many people share responsibility for this problem. For every ineffective teacher who is now in charge of a classroom, there are several school officials who told him or her: we want you to teach; we want you to take a job in *this* school, teaching *these* students; we want you to receive tenure. Every unsuccessful teacher was recruited, hired, assigned to a particular grade level and course, evaluated, and tenured by school officials—officials whose actions were authorized and supported by elected representatives of the people. No teachers forced their way into the school system. Thus, the responsibility for poor teaching lies squarely on the shoulders of the long-established system of teacher hiring, placement, and promotion.

School districts have chosen to employ teachers who are not effective for several reasons:

- the simple need to have a "warm body" in front of every classroomful of students, in years when low teacher salaries make it impossible to attract skilled teachers;
- an unwillingness to raise taxes to pay the salaries required to attract better applicants;*
- an unwillingness to spend money on a personnel system capable of evaluating applicants critically (including observing applicants' performance in practice teaching situations or in their current classrooms);
- reliance on centralized teacher hiring and placement procedures, instead of involving principals and teachers in the selection of good teachers for their school; and
- schools officials' unwillingness to spend the time required to document a teacher's incompetent performance as grounds for dismissal (this management option is available in every school district, and continues to offer a solution to the problem of ineffective teachers in some instances).

This list makes it clear that it is simply foolish to blame teachers—either individually or as a group—for school officials' inappropriate hiring and other personnel decisions. Instead of blaming teachers, we need to find management tactics that can remedy the problem.

---

*Before the mid-1960s, it was relatively easy for school districts to hire smart, skilled women for low-paying teaching jobs because they had few alternative job opportunities; this is no longer true. Today, good salaries are required to attract good teachers.[3]

For those teachers who do not improve with training and a different classroom assignment, new approaches are needed. One method of replacing ineffective teachers is for school districts to facilitate voluntary early retirements. Being an unsuccessful teacher is no fun; there are constant, painful, daily reminders of one's shortcomings. The vulnerability of people in classrooms guarantees that all teachers receive lots of feedback on whether things are going well or badly in their classroom. While some unsuccessful teachers have such poor prospects for employment outside the schools that they choose to remain in their jobs despite daily failure, it is also likely that many teachers who perceive themselves to be unsuccessful simply leave teaching on their own. (Sadly, those who leave teaching doubtlessly include some teachers who could have been successful had they been given classrooms well matched to their skills and preparation.)

Early retirement plans and career-change subsidies would allow teachers who want to leave teaching to do so without having to absorb the large short-term transition cost themselves. It will be necessary to negotiate the details of these arrangements with teachers' union representatives, to guard against the possibility that school officials would unfairly pressure teachers who are thorns in the administration's side to leave their jobs.[4] Such collectively bargained programs could smooth the way for unsuccessful teachers to leave the classroom, subsidized by the management that got them hired in the first place.

No strategy to reduce the number of ineffective teachers will work unless those who depart are replaced by more effective teachers, and there is reason to doubt that this will happen unless current hiring practices are changed. A successful strategy would combine several approaches: management that matches teachers to classrooms in which they can be successful; higher salaries, reliably sustained over time; and improved recruitment, hiring, and evaluation practices (including classroom observation of teachers before hiring, and information from principals and teachers on applicants' suitability for a particular school). Until these changes in school personnel systems are in place, the net quality of the teacher labor force will not improve.

Every discussion of new teacher policies hinges on a key political issue: the question of which level of government will take responsibility for making the necessary changes. Increases in individual school districts' salary scales will not motivate large numbers of potential teaching applicants to change their behavior. The lump-sum costs of early retirement and career-change subsidies are beyond the fiscal capacity of most local school districts. These considerations point to state governments as the logical source of effective teacher policies. Yet because the states vary in their politics and their wealth, strong federal incentives (perhaps in the form of matching grants) will be needed to induce some states to improve their teacher policies. Such a federal policy will benefit all states, because the children who are taught in low-quality schools often move to other states after their education is ended. At bottom, however, the capacity of higher teacher salaries to improve the schools will depend on local hiring decisions, assignments of teachers to specific classrooms, and the work that they do in those classrooms.

So far, this discussion has mostly focused on ineffective teachers who are unable to improve. Probably a far larger cause of poor-quality teaching is the assignment of teachers to classes that they should not be teaching, a practice common in school districts where enrollments (and thus job slots for current teachers) are declining. A teacher who is unsuccessful when assigned to teach in a field outside his or her expertise might well succeed if given a more appropriate teaching assignment. Many school districts also thwart teacher success through the destructive practice of assigning new teachers to classrooms containing high concentrations of difficult-to-teach children, while experienced teachers teach in less demanding classrooms.

Sensibly matching teachers with courses and students can give teachers the opportunity to improve their effectiveness virtually overnight. No teacher can be adequate to the needs of every child, and finding a better classroom placement for certain children may suddenly allow a teacher to be effective. Other teachers' work might be dramatically improved by some pointed and specific training. These examples suggest that if school officials become more involved in solving *classroom* problems—and particularly in matching teachers to the students they can teach most effectively—the number of unsuccessful teachers can be sharply reduced.

Classroom Information as the Key Incentive for Change

For the education system to solve its problems, its leaders need clear, usable information about where and how the system is failing and how its failures can be fixed. This book's arguments point toward the information that is needed: *classroom* information. While information on the problems of individual classrooms is likely to be complicated, thorny, and difficult to interpret, it directly reflects the success of teaching and learning, by identifying problems in the settings that do the most to shape teaching and learning. As the experiences of Newton and Berkeley demonstrate, classroom information can push school officials to respond to incorrect classroom assignments, ineffective teaching, discipline problems, and academic failure. If we are to improve the schools, we must elicit new information about the success or failure of individual classrooms—and use that information as the basis for our actions.

The best sources of information on classrooms are teachers, students, and parents. Their involvement in the classroom assignment process can not only improve the match between teachers and students, but will also help inform school officials about which classrooms work, which don't, and what measures are needed to fix the latter. When people in classrooms press their information onto the agenda of school officials and policy makers, they will stimulate those officials to pay attention to their classrooms' problems, forcefully reminding them of the importance of hiring and tenure decisions, classroom assignment decisions, and interventions by the principal in classrooms to which parents do not want their children assigned. By increasing the school system's use of information on the quality of teaching and learning in each of its classrooms, the Newton Solution turns classroom information into the key incentive for educational changes that benefit all students.

Other kinds of classroom information can stimulate changes in education policy, too. School officials can monitor key classroom indicators: classroom achievement gains, attendance levels, and parent complaints. They can offer minigrants for teachers' classroom initiatives, thus stimulating classroom-level solutions to teaching and learning problems. They can use classroom information as the basis for ad hoc actions tailored to solve particular classroom problems. Classroom information is a valuable commodity. It pushes school officials in the right direction: toward dealing with ineffective teachers, improving classroom assignments, and responding to classroom problems. It constantly underscores the fact that society should not accept failing classrooms for *anyone*. Currently, classroom information is possessed by teachers, students, and parents—but there are few incentives for school officials to use their information to improve the schools. When parents and teachers become involved in the classroom assignment process, their actions will create the incentives for school officials to pay attention to classroom information.

The great, but little noticed, discovery of education policy research is this: students' achievement is determined by the classroom to which they belong. This simple fact shows the central mistake of the education policy debate; it has ignored the classroom crucible, the productive core of schooling. The policy debate has treated the people in classrooms as underlings who are supposed to follow procedures that are established by others. This is, quite simply, crazy. Until school officials, policy makers, and parents learn to base their decisions on the realities of life in the classroom—on the issues facing the teachers and students who make education happen every day—education policies will continue to fail. The success of education requires education policies that strengthen the ability of teachers and students to make their classrooms work. In the end, we must rely on the people in classrooms to carry out the work of education—not because they will always do it well, but because they are the only ones who can do it at all.

NOTES

INTRODUCTION

1. See Harvey A. Averch et al., *How Effective Is Schooling? A Critical Review of Research* (Englewood Cliffs, N. J.: Educational Technology Publications, 1974), p. 171; and John F. Witte, "Understanding High School Achievement: After a Decade of Research, Do We Have Any Confident Policy Recommendations?" paper presented at the annual meeting of the American Political Science Association, September, 1990.
2. David B. Tyack, *The One Best System: A History of American Urban Education* (Cambridge: Harvard University Press, 1974). Tyack describes the search for the "one best system" of management for the schools, based on centralized control and imitating the control system used in private corporations; see esp. pp. 126–76.
3. Seymour B. Sarason, *The Culture of the School and the Problem of Change* (Boston: Allyn and Bacon, 1971; 2d ed. 1982); Philip W. Jackson, *Life in Classrooms* (New York: Holt, Rinehart and Winston, 1968); Dan C. Lortie, *Schoolteacher: A Sociological Study* (Chicago: University of Chicago Press, 1975); Joseph

Featherstone, "Books Considered: Schooling in Capitalist America by Samuel Bowles and Herbert Gintis," *The New Republic* 74 (May 29, 1976): 26–29.

4. See, for example, National Commission on Excellence in Education, *A Nation at Risk: The Imperative for Educational Reform* (Washington, D.C.: U.S. Department of Education, 1983); and U.S. Department of Education, *The Nation Responds: Recent Efforts to Improve Education* (Washington, D.C.: U.S. Department of Education, 1984). These documents were commissioned by the Reagan administration.

5. See, for example, Carnegie Forum on Education and the Economy, *A Nation Prepared: Teachers for the 21st Century* (New York: Carnegie Corporation, 1986); and Commission on Work, Family, and Citizenship, *The Forgotten Half: Non-College Youth in America* (Washington, D.C.: William T. Grant Foundation, 1988). The Carnegie recommendations include increased teacher salaries, improved and expanded teacher training, and increased teacher involvement in school decision making. The Grant recommendations call for expansions of Head Start, Chapter 1, and vocational education programs for children who are not going to attend college.

6. Seymour B. Sarason and John Doris, *Educational Handicap, Public Policy, and Social History* (New York: Free Press, 1979), chap. 10, "Immigration and Educational Problems in the Nineteenth Century," pp. 183–206.

7. Diane Ravitch, *The Great School Wars: New York City, 1805–1973* (New York: Basic Books, 1974), chaps. 11–15.

8. Tyack, pp. 128–29. See also Raymond E. Callahan, *Education and the Cult of Efficiency* (Chicago: University of Chicago Press, 1962), chaps. 1, 5.

9. Lawrence A. Cremin, *American Education: The Metropolitan Experience, 1876–1980* (New York: Harper & Row, 1988), p. 228.

10. U.S. Department of Education, *The Nation Responds.*

11. Nancy Mathis, "In Finance Arena, a New Activism Emerges," *Education Week* 8 (31 [April 26, 1989]): 1, 8–11.

12. Eric A. Hanushek, "Throwing Money at Schools," *Journal of Policy Analysis and Management* 1 (1981): 19–41. The evidence on policy proposals based on new controls, such as merit pay

for teachers, is similarly discouraging; see, for example, David K. Cohen and Richard J. Murnane, "The Merits of Merit Pay," *The Public Interest,* No. 80 (Summer, 1985), pp. 3–30. Evidence on the ineffectiveness of education policies is discussed in detail in chapter 6 of this book.

13. The evidence on the causes of student achievement declines in the 1960s and 1970s, and achievement gains since then is in Daniel Koretz, *Educational Achievement: Explanations and Implications of Recent Trends* (Washington, D.C.: Congressional Budget Office, 1987), pp. xi–xii, 30, 36.

14. Rebecca Barr and Robert Dreeben, *How Schools Work* (Chicago: University of Chicago Press, 1983), pp. 7, 9–10.

CHAPTER 1

1. James S. Coleman and Ernest Q. Campbell, Carol J. Hobson, James McPartland, Alexander M. Mood, Frederic D. Weinfeld, Robert L. York, *Equality of Educational Opportunity* (Washington, D.C.: National Center for Educational Statistics, 1966), chap. 3.1, "Outcomes of Schooling," pp. 218–90.

2. Ibid., chap. 2.2, "School Facilities, Services, and Curriculums," pp. 66–122.

3. Ibid., chap. 3.2, "Relation of School Factors to Achievement," pp. 290–330.

4. Ibid., chap. 3.22, "School-to-School Variations in Achievement," pp. 295–302.

5. Ibid., p. 296.

6. Ibid.

7. Frederick Mosteller and Daniel P. Moynihan, "A Pathbreaking Report," in Mosteller and Moynihan, eds., *On Equality of Educational Opportunity* (New York: Random House, 1972), p. 21; Christopher Jencks, Marshall Smith, Henry Acland, Mary Jo Bane, David K. Cohen, Herbert Gintis, Barbara Heyns, and Stephan Michelson, *Inequality: A Reassessment of the Effect of Family and Schooling in America* (New York: Basic Books, 1972), pp. 85–89: "The Effects of School Attendance."

8. The quotation is from Rebecca Barr and Robert Dreeben, *How*

Schools Work (Chicago: University of Chicago Press, 1983), p. 166.

9. Ibid., pp. 113, 166.
10. Coleman et al., *Educational Opportunity,* p. 325.
11. Jencks et al., *Inequality,* pp. 146–47, "The Effects of School Quality on Educational Attainment."
12. Ibid., pp. 296–97.
13. For example, David K. Cohen, Thomas F. Pettigrew, and Robert T. Riley, "Race and the Outcomes of Schooling," and Mosteller and Moynihan, "Pathbreaking Report," in Mosteller and Moynihan, eds., *On Equality of Educational Opportunity,* pp. 343–68; 28–32.
14. Coleman et al., *Educational Opportunity,* pp. 295–96; Coleman, "The Evaluation of *Equality of Educational Opportunity,*" in Mosteller and Moynihan, eds., *On Equality of Educational Opportunity,* pp. 146–67.
15. Paul Berman and Milbrey Wallin McLaughlin, *Federal Programs Supporting Educational Change,* vol. 1, *A Model of Educational Change* (Santa Monica, Calif.: Rand Corporation, 1974), chap. 2, "Literature on Educational Innovations: Project and Policy Studies," pp. 3–6.
16. Fritz J. Roethlisberger, *Management and the Worker* (Cambridge: Harvard University Press, 1939); and F. Roethlisberger, *Management and Morale* (Cambridge: Harvard University Press, 1941).
17. Mosteller and Moynihan, "Pathbreaking Report," pp. 4, 8–12, 15–24, 27–28.
18. Henry S. Dyer, "Some Thoughts About Future Studies," in Mosteller and Moynihan, eds., *On Equality of Educational Opportunity,* pp. 384–422.
19. Eric A. Hanushek and John F. Kain, "On the Value of *Equality of Educational Opportunity* as a Guide to Public Policy," in Mosteller and Moynihan, eds., *On Equality of Educational Opportunity,* pp. 116–45.
20. Eric A. Hanushek, *Education and Race: An Analysis of the Educational Production Process* (Lexington, Mass.: D.C. Heath, 1972), chap. 3. Other descriptions of this research, in which Hanushek presents more thorough conceptual and methodological explanations of his work, appear in Eric A. Hanushek,

The Value of Teachers in Teaching (Santa Monica, Calif.: Rand Corporation, 1970); and E. Hanushek, "Teacher Characteristics and Gains in Student Achievement: Estimation Using Micro-Data," *American Economic Review* 61 (May, 1971): 280–88. Hanushek expands on the significance of his methodological decisions in "Conceptual and Empirical Issues in the Estimation of Educational Production Functions," *Journal of Human Resources* 14 (Summer, 1979): 351–88.

21. Hanushek, *Education and Race,* chap. 3.
22. Ibid., p. 51.
23. See David Armor, Patricia Conry-Oseguera, Millicent Cox, Nicelma King, Lorraine McDonnell, Anthony Pascal, Edward Pauly, and Gail Zellman, *Analysis of the School Preferred Reading Program in Selected Los Angeles Minority Schools* (Santa Monica, Calif.: Rand Corporation, 1976), chap. 3, pp. 17–35.
24. Richard J. Murnane, *The Impact of School Resources on the Learning of Inner City Children* (Cambridge, Mass.: Ballinger, 1975).
25. Rebecca A. Maynard and Richard J. Murnane, "The Effects of a Negative Income Tax on School Performance: Results of an Experiment," *Journal of Human Resources* 14 (Fall, 1979): 463–76.
26. Chap. 3, "Influence of School and Classroom Factors on Reading Achievement," in David Armor et al., *School Preferred Reading Program,* pp. 17–35.
27. The data supporting these conclusions are the same as those reported in Murnane, *Impact of School Resources.*
28. Armor et al., *School Preferred Reading Program.*
29. Richard J. Murnane, "Interpreting the Evidence on School Effectiveness," *Teachers College Record* 83 (Fall, 1981): 20.
30. Eric A. Hanushek, "Throwing Money at Schools," *Journal of Policy Analysis and Management* 1 (1981): 30.
31. Anonymous superintendent, interview, 1989.

CHAPTER 2

1. Philip W. Jackson, *Life in Classrooms* (New York: Holt, Rinehart and Winston, 1968), p. 8.
2. Ibid., chap. 1, "The Daily Grind," pp. 1–37.

3. See Willard Waller, *The Sociology of Teaching* (New York: John Wiley and Sons, 1932), pp. 297–304.

4. See Gertrude H. McPherson, *Small Town Teacher* (Cambridge: Harvard University Press, 1972), pp. 110–19.

5. See Seymour B. Sarason, *The Culture of the School and the Problem of Change,* 2d ed. (Boston: Allyn and Bacon, 1982), chap. 11, "The Teacher: Constitutional Issues in the Classroom," pp. 215–20.

6. Jackson, *Life in Classrooms,* esp. pp. 86–102.

7. Jo Michelle Beld Fraatz, *The Politics of Reading: Power, Opportunity, and Prospects for Change in America's Public Schools* (New York: Teachers College Press, 1987), pp. 44–45.

8. Waller, *Sociology of Teaching,* pp. 137–38, 150.

9. Katherine Nelson, "Social Cognition in a Script Framework," mimeo, Department of Psychology, City University of New York Graduate Center, n.d., pp. 10–15.

CHAPTER 3

1. Jack H. Nagel, *The Descriptive Analysis of Power* (New Haven: Yale University Press, 1975); for Nagel's comments on people who deny that power is present in certain systems, see p. 178. Among Nagel's sources for his analysis of power was the concept of control developed by Robert A. Dahl and Charles E. Lindblom in *Politics, Economics, and Welfare* (New York: Harper & Row, 1953), p. 94. See also Robert A. Dahl, "Power," in David L. Sills, ed., *International Encyclopedia of the Social Sciences,* vol. 12 (New York: Macmillan and Free Press, 1968), pp. 405–15.

2. See Gertrude H. McPherson, *Small Town Teacher* (Cambridge: Harvard University Press, 1972), p. 109.

3. Ibid.

4. Nagel, *Analysis of Power,* chap. 9, "Symmetry and Asymmetry in Power Relations," p. 142.

5. Richard E. Neustadt, *Presidential Power: The Politics of Leadership* (New York: John Wiley and Sons, 1960), pp. 42, 51.

6. Carl Milofsky, *Special Education: A Sociological Study of California Programs* (New York: Praeger, 1976), pp. 98–108; see esp. chap. 5, "Student Lawyers."

7. John I. Goodlad, *A Place Called School: Prospects for the Future* (New York: McGraw-Hill, 1984), p. 186.

8. The idea of feedback has its roots in the work of Norbert Wiener; see his *The Human Use of Human Beings* (Boston: Houghton Mifflin, 1950). The anticipation of other people's reactions, and the resulting influence on the person who does the anticipating, is discussed as a form of power by many political scientists, summarized in Robert A. Dahl, *Modern Political Analysis,* 2d ed. (Englewood Cliffs, N.J.: Prentice-Hall, 1984), p. 25.

9. Jo Michelle Beld Fraatz, *The Politics of Reading: Power, Opportunity, and Prospects for Change in America's Public Schools* (New York: Teachers College Press, 1987); see esp. "Power and Opportunity in the Classroom," pp. 31–32.

10. See Elizabeth Janeway, *Powers of the Weak* (New York: Alfred A. Knopf, 1980).

11. Seymour B. Sarason, *The Culture of the School and the Problem of Change,* 2d ed. (Boston: Allyn and Bacon, 1982), p. 71.

12. Ann Lieberman, "Practice Makes Policy: The Tensions of School Improvement," in A. Lieberman and M. W. McLaughlin, eds., *Policy Making in Education,* Yearbook of the National Society for the Study of Education (Chicago: University of Chicago Press, 1982), p. 25.

13. Richard J. Murnane and Richard R. Nelson, "Production and Innovation When Techniques Are Tacit: The Case of Education," *Journal of Economic Behavior and Organization* 5 (1984): 359, 360.

14. Jeanne S. Chall, *Learning to Read: The Great Debate* (New York: McGraw-Hill, 1967), p. 284.

15. Ibid.

CHAPTER 4

1. Paul Berman and Milbrey Wallin McLaughlin, *Federal Programs Supporting Educational Change,* vol. 1, *A Model of Educational Change* (Santa Monica, Calif.: Rand Corporation, 1974), p. 4; Ford Foundation, *A Foundation Goes to School: The Ford Foundation Comprehensive School Improvement Program, 1960–1970*

(New York: Ford Foundation Office of Reports, 1972); D. G. Hawkridge, G. K. Tallmadge, and J. K. Larsen, *Foundations for Success in Educating Disadvantaged Children* (Palo Alto, Calif.: American Institutes for Research, 1968).

2. Lynn Olson and Blake Rodman, "In the Urban Crucible: Teachers and Students Struggle With an Indifferent System that 'Grinds Them Up,' " *Education Week* 7 (June 22, 1988): 28.

3. Richard J. Murnane, *The Impact of School Resources on the Learning of Inner City Children* (Cambridge, Mass.: Ballinger, 1975), pp. 40, 69, and tables.

4. Carol Ascher, "Improving Chapter 1 Delivery," *ERIC Clearinghouse on Urban Education Digest* 39 (January, 1988): 1ff. Ascher cites several studies of Chapter 1 programs that use the "pullout" method (removing students from their classroom for remedial instruction), including M. S. Knapp, B. J. Turnbull, et al., "Local Program Design and Decision Making under Chapter 1 of the Education Consolidation and Improvement Act" (Menlo Park, Calif.: SRI International, 1986).

5. Richard J. Murnane and Richard R. Nelson, "Production and Innovation When Techniques Are Tacit: The Case of Education," *Journal of Economic Behavior and Organization* 5 (1984): 353–73; see esp. pp. 368–71.

6. See Howard Gardner, *Frames of Mind: The Theory of Multiple Intelligences* (New York: Basic Books, 1983), for a discussion of "interpersonal intelligence," p. 239 and chap. 10.

7. Ibid., pp. 368–69.

8. James G. March and Herbert A. Simon, *Organizations* (New York: John Wiley and Sons, 1958), pp. 172–210.

9. See Arthur G. Powell, Eleanor Farrar, and David K. Cohen, *The Shopping Mall High School: Winners and Losers in the Educational Marketplace* (Boston: Houghton Mifflin, 1985).

10. Murnane and Nelson, "The Case of Education," p. 370.

CHAPTER 5

1. William Snider, "Study Examines Forces Affecting Racial Tracking; Findings Drawn from Survey of 173 Districts," *Education Week* 8 (November 11, 1987): 1, 20.

2. Lynn Olson, "Effective Schools," *Education Week* 5 (January 15, 1986): 11–21.

3. Ibid.

4. Peter W. Greenwood, Dale Mann, and Milbrey Wallin McLaughlin, *Federal Programs Supporting Educational Change*, vol. 3, *The Process of Change* (Santa Monica, Calif.: Rand Corporation, 1975), p. 38.

CHAPTER 6

1. The study appeared in book form as Harvey A. Averch, Stephen J. Carroll, Theodore S. Donaldson, Herbert J. Kiesling, and John Pincus, *How Effective Is Schooling? A Critical Review of Research* (Englewood Cliffs, N. J.: Educational Technology Publications, 1974); see p. 171.

2. Ibid., p. 172.

3. Paul Berman and Milbrey Wallin McLaughlin, *Federal Programs Supporting Educational Change*, vol. 8, *Implementing and Sustaining Innovations* (Santa Monica, Calif.: Rand Corporation, 1978), p. 1.

4. Diane Ravitch, *The Troubled Crusade: American Education 1945–1980* (New York: Basic Books, 1983), p. 317.

5. Arthur E. Wise, *Legislated Learning: The Bureaucratization of the American Classroom* (Berkeley: University of California Press, 1979).

6. Ravitch, *Troubled Crusade*, p. 312, quoting Wise, *Legislated Learning*, p. 2.

7. Jeanne S. Chall, *Learning to Read: The Great Debate* (New York: McGraw-Hill, 1967), pp. 284–85; David T. Kearns and Denis P. Doyle, *Winning the Brain Race: A Bold Plan to Make Our Schools Competitive* (San Francisco: ICS Press, 1988), pp. 52ff.

8. Averch et al., *How Effective is Schooling?* pp. 171–72; Paul Berman and Milbrey Wallin McLaughlin, *Federal Programs Supporting Educational Change*, vol. 1, *A Model of Educational Change* (Santa Monica, Calif.: Rand Corporation, 1974), pp. 1, 3, 4; Berman and McLaughlin, *Federal Programs*, vol. 8, pp. 1–2; Eric A. Hanushek, "Throwing Money at Schools," *Journal of Policy Analysis and Management* 1 (1981): 20, 37; John F.

220 *Notes*

Witte, "Understanding High School Achievement: After a Decade of Research, Do We Have Any Confident Policy Recommendations?" paper presented at the annual meeting of the American Political Science Association, September 1990.

9. Hanushek, "Throwing Money at Schools," p. 37.
10. Wise, *Legislated Learning*.
11. Berman and McLaughlin, *Federal Programs,* vol. 8.
12. Various authors, *Federal Programs Supporting Educational Change,* vols. 1–8 and appendices (Santa Monica, Calif.: Rand Corporation, 1974–1978).
13. Berman and McLaughlin, vol. 1, pp. 8–22.
14. Ibid., vol. 8, p. 16.
15. Arthur Blumberg and William Greenfield, *The Effective Principal: Perspectives on School Leadership,* 2d ed. (Boston: Allyn and Bacon, 1986), p. 142.
16. Peter W. Greenwood, Dale Mann, and Milbrey Wallin McLaughlin, *Federal Programs Supporting Educational Change,* vol. 3, *The Process of Change* (Santa Monica, Calif.: Rand Corporation, 1975).
17. Berman and McLaughlin, *Federal Programs,* vol. 1, p. 10.
18. Ibid., vol. 8, p. 37; see also pp. 15–16.
19. Carol VanDeusen Lukas, "Problems in Implementing Head Start Planned Variation Models," in Alice M. Rivlin and P. Michael Timpane, eds., *Planned Variation in Education: Should We Give Up or Try Harder?* (Washington, D.C.: Brookings Institution, 1975), pp. 113–25.
20. Ibid., pp. 118–19.
21. Seymour B. Sarason, *The Culture of the School and the Problem of Change* (Boston: Allyn and Bacon, 1971), pp. 45–61, 86–87; Paul Berman and Milbrey Wallin McLaughlin, *Federal Programs Supporting Educational Change,* vol. 4, *The Findings in Review* (Santa Monica, Calif.: Rand Corporation, 1975); ibid., vol. 8; Greenwood, Mann, and McLaughlin, *Federal Programs,* vol. 3; Lukas, "Implementing Head Start"; Chall, *Learning to Read,* p. 284.
22. Robert Rothman, "Teacher vs. Curriculum in Philadelphia?" *Education Week* 7 (March 23, 1988): 1, 20–22. The survey analyzed in detail the response of Philadelphia teachers to a new prescribed curriculum introduced by the school district.

The study was by Gail B. Raznov, an instructional coordinator at Gratz High School.

23. Berman and McLaughlin, *Federal Programs,* vol. 8, pp. 40–41, 43–44; Lukas, "Implementing Head Start"; David Armor et al., *Analysis of the School Preferred Reading Program in Selected Los Angeles Minority Schools* (Santa Monica, Calif.: Rand Corporation, 1976), pp. 28, 39.

24. Thomas B. Timar and David L. Kirp, *Managing Educational Excellence* (Philadelphia: Falmer Press, 1988), p. 93.

25. Milton Friedman, *Capitalism and Freedom* (Chicago: University of Chicago Press, 1962), pp. 85–107. See also John Chubb and Terry Moe, *Politics, Markets, and America's Schools* (Washington, D.C.: Brookings Books, 1990), for a detailed analysis of a choice proposal.

26. Richard J. Murnane, "Interpreting the Evidence on School Effectiveness," *Teachers College Record* 83 (Fall, 1981): 33.

27. Richard J. Murnane, *The Impact of School Resources on the Learning of Inner City Children* (Cambridge, Mass.: Ballinger, 1975), pp. 63–75, 78.

28. Lynn Olson and Blake Rodman, "In the Urban Crucible: Teachers and Students Struggle With an Indifferent System that 'Grinds Them Up,' " *Education Week* 7 (June 22, 1988): 29–30.

29. Sarason, *Culture of the School,* chaps. 8, 9, 12.

30. Berman and McLaughlin, *Federal Programs,* vol. 8, pp. 30–31.

31. Harry F. Wolcott, *The Man in the Principal's Office: An Ethnography* (New York: Holt, Rinehart and Winston, 1973), chap. 6, "What a Principal Does: Informal Encounters and Daily Routines," and chap. 9, "Maintaining the System: The Principal as Socializer"; and Dan C. Lortie, *Schoolteacher: A Sociological Study* (Chicago: University of Chicago Press, 1975), pp. 197–203.

32. Jane Perlez, "New Principal Calms a Troubled School," *New York Times,* 6 April 1988, pp. B1, B4.

33. Jo Michelle Beld Fraatz, *The Politics of Reading* (New York: Teachers College Press, 1987), chap. 3, "Reading Specialists and the Mobilization of Bias," and chap. 4, "The Power of Suggestion? Elementary School Principals, Effectiveness, and Equality," pp. 66–125.

34. Arthur G. Powell, Eleanor Farrar, and David K. Cohen, *The Shopping Mall High School: Winners and Losers in the Educational Marketplace* (Boston: Houghton Mifflin, 1985).

35. William Snider, " 'Small Changes' Won't Do, Says California Panel: Cites Failure To Serve Diverse Student Body," *Education Week* 7 (June 8, 1988): 1, 12.

36. Isaiah Berlin, "On the Pursuit of the Ideal," *New York Review of Books*, 17 March 1988, pp. 11–18.

37. A. Grant Jordan, "Pluralism," in Vernon Bogdanor, ed., *Blackwell Encyclopedia of Political Institutions* (Oxford: Basil Blackwell, 1987), pp. 426–8.

38. Armor et al., *School Preferred Reading Program*.

CHAPTER 7

1. Liese Klein, "School's Out," *New Haven Advocate*, 5 December 1988, pp. 1, 8.

2. Esther K. Sarason and Seymour B. Sarason, "Some Observations on the Introduction and Teaching of the New Math," in Frances Kaplan and Seymour B. Sarason, eds., *The Psycho-Educational Clinic: Papers and Research Studies* (Boston: Massachusetts Department of Mental Health, 1969), pp. 91–107.

3. Milbrey Wallin McLaughlin, *Evaluation and Reform: The Elementary and Secondary Education Act of 1965, Title I* (Cambridge, Mass.: Ballinger, 1975).

4. Paul Berman and Milbrey Wallin McLaughlin, *Federal Programs Supporting Educational Change*, vol. 4, *The Findings in Review* (Santa Monica, Calif.: Rand Corporation, 1975), p. 25.

5. Richard J. Murnane and Randall J. Olsen, "The Effects of Salaries and Opportunity Costs on Duration in Teaching: Evidence from Michigan," *Review of Economics and Statistics* 11 (2 [1989]): 347–52.

6. David M. Grether and Peter Mieszkowski, "Determinants of Real-Estate Values," *Journal of Urban Economics* 1 (1974): 127–46.

7. Richard J. Murnane, "Evidence, Analysis, and Unanswered Questions," *Harvard Educational Review* 51 (November, 1981): 483–89.

8. Richard J. Murnane, "Interpreting the Evidence on School Effectiveness," *Teachers College Record* 83 (Fall, 1981): 19–35; Richard J. Murnane, "Understanding the Sources of Teaching Competence: Choices, Skills, and the Limits of Training," *Teachers College Record* 84 (3 [Spring, 1983]): 564–69; Richard J. Murnane, "Family Choice in Public Education: The Roles of Students, Teachers, and System Designers," *Teachers College Record* 88 (Winter, 1986): 169–89; Sarason and Sarason, "Teaching of New Math"; McLaughlin, *Evaluation and Reform;* Berman and McLaughlin, *Federal Programs,* vols. 4, 8.

9. Murnane, "School Effectiveness," p. 33.

10. This analysis benefited from my discussions with Seymour Sarason. He first wrote about it in Seymour B. Sarason, Murray Levine, Ira I. Goldenberg, Dennis L. Cherlin, and E. Bennett, *Psychology in Community Settings* (New York: John Wiley and Sons, 1966).

11. See William Snider, "Conceding Failure, Fernandez Orders Dropout Initiative," *Education Week* 9 (May 23, 1990): 1, 10. The article cited an unpublished study by Joseph C. Grannis.

12. Richard J. Murnane, *The Impact of School Resources on the Learning of Inner City Children* (Cambridge, Mass.: Ballinger, 1975), pp. 69, 78.

13. Richard J. Murnane, Judith D. Singer, John B. Willett, James J. Kemple, and Randall J. Olsen, *Who Will Teach: Policies That Matter* (Cambridge: Harvard University Press, forthcoming, 1991); Murnane and Olsen, "Opportunity Costs"; Richard J. Murnane and Randall J. Olsen, "Factors Affecting Length of Stay in Teaching: Evidence from North Carolina," *Journal of Human Resources* 25 (Winter, 1990): 106–24; Charles F. Manski, "Academic Ability, Earnings, and the Decision to Become a Teacher: Evidence from the National Longitudinal Study of the Class of 1972," in David A. Wise, ed., *Public Sector Payrolls* (Chicago: University of Chicago Press, 1987); Peter Dolton, "The Economics of U.K. Teacher Supply: The Graduate's Decision," *Economic Journal* 100 (1990): 91–104.

14. Arthur E. Wise, Linda Darling-Hammond, and Barnett Berry, *Effective Teacher Selection: From Recruitment to Retention* (Santa Monica, Calif.: Rand Corporation, 1987), pp. 86–88.

15. Milbrey Wallin McLaughlin et al., "Why Teachers Won't

Teach," *Phi Delta Kappan* 67 (1986): 424; Susan Moore Johnson, *Teachers at Work: Achieving Success in Our Schools* (New York: Basic Books, 1990).

16. Nat Hentoff, *Village Voice*, 24 March 1987, p. 27; Deborah Meier quoted in William Snider, "Convergence on Choice," *Teacher Magazine* 1 (February, 1990): 18–20.

17. David Greenberg and John McCall, "Teacher Mobility and Allocation," *Journal of Human Resources* 9 (Fall, 1974): 480–502; Wise, Darling-Hammond, and Berry, *Effective Teacher Selection*, pp. 90–91.

18. Seymour B. Sarason, *The Culture of the School and the Problem of Change*, 2d ed. (Boston: Allyn and Bacon, 1982), chap. 9, "The Principal and the Use of 'The System,' " pp. 163–84.

19. David Armor et al., *Analysis of the School Preferred Reading Program in Selected Los Angeles Minority Schools* (Santa Monica, Calif.: Rand Corporation, 1976), p. 28.

20. Arthur G. Powell, Eleanor Farrar, and David K. Cohen, *The Shopping Mall High School: Winners and Losers in the Educational Marketplace* (Boston: Houghton Mifflin, 1985).

21. See Roland S. Barth, *Improving Schools From Within: Teachers, Parents, and Principals Can Make the Difference* (San Francisco: Jossey-Bass, 1990).

22. James P. Comer, *School Power: Implications of an Intervention Project* (New York: Free Press, 1980); James P. Comer, "Educating Poor Minority Children," *Scientific American* 259 (November, 1988): 42–48.

23. Lorraine McDonnell and Milbrey Wallin McLaughlin, *Program Consolidation and the State Role in ESEA, Title IV* (Santa Monica, Calif.: Rand Corporation, 1980).

24. Peter W. Greenwood, Dale Mann, and Milbrey Wallin McLaughlin, *Federal Programs Supporting Educational Change*, vol. 3, *The Process of Change* (Santa Monica, Calif.: Rand Corporation, 1975).

25. See the general treatment of related ideas in Charles E. Lindblom and David K. Cohen, *Usable Knowledge: Social Science and Social Problem Solving* (New Haven: Yale University Press, 1979).

26. See, for example, the experiences recounted in Rosalie Ped-

alino Porter, *Forked Tongue: The Politics of Bilingual Education* (New York: Basic Books, 1990).

27. One version of this proposal has been put forward by the American Federation of Teachers. See Albert Shanker, "A Charter for Change," *Education Week* 7 (August 3, 1988): 26.
28. See Note 22.

CHAPTER 8

1. Roland S. Barth, *Run School Run* (Cambridge: Harvard University Press, 1980), pp. 60–61.
2. Barth, interview, May 31, 1990.
3. Barth, *Run School Run,* pp. 83–84.
4. David Michaud, Director of Elementary Education, Newton, Massachusetts, interview, June 15, 1990. Michaud also notes that principals in Newton vary in how much they encourage parents to make their preferences known.
5. Clifford Wong, Associate Superintendent of Schools, Berkeley, California, interview, May 14, 1990. I am also indebted to Ronald Kemper, president of the Berkeley school board, for information on classroom assignment policies in Berkeley.
6. Ibid.
7. David H. Monk, "Assigning Elementary Pupils to Their Teachers," *The Elementary School Journal* 88 (2 [November, 1987]), pp. 174–76, 179.
8. Barth, *Run School Run,* pp. 57–58, 74.
9. Monk, p. 178.
10. These characteristics are based on the author's teacher and parent interviews, and on examples discussed in Barth, *Run School Run,* pp. 51–93.
11. Monk, p. 178.
12. Ibid.
13. Ibid., pp. 170–71.
14. Wong, interview. (See Note 5.)
15. Sara Lawrence Lightfoot, *Worlds Apart: Relationships Between Families and Schools* (New York: Basic Books, 1978). Lightfoot examines in detail the perceptions of mothers and teachers

about the children whose lives they share, and about each other; she shows that these perceptions are frequently tinged with suspicion and hostility.

16. Barth, *Run School Run*, pp. 80–81.
17. Wong, interview. (See Note 5.)
18. See Albert O. Hirschman, *Exit, Voice, and Loyalty: Responses to Decline in Firms, Organizations, and States* (Cambridge: Harvard University Press, 1970). Hirschman's deservedly famous book argues that economists and policy makers have erred by ignoring the beneficial effects of "voice" (that is, consumer complaints about poor quality products and services), which can be as important a source of organizational change as "exit" (that is, consumer decisions not to patronize a poor quality organization). Moreover, voice can be combined with exit: ". . . once voice is recognized as a mechanism with considerable usefulness for maintaining performance, institutions can be designed in such a way that the cost of individual and collective action would be decreased . . . [by raising] the general readiness of a population to complain and . . . [creating] such institutions and mechanisms as can communicate complaints cheaply and effectively" (pp. 42–43). When parents request a particular classroom assignment for their child, they are combining voice (the request, and their stated reasons for it) with the possibility of exit (due to their dissatisfaction with other potential classroom assignments). Increased parent involvement in classroom assignment decisions would cheaply and effectively add to the use of voice in public school systems.
19. Richard J. Murnane, *The Impact of School Resources on the Learning of Inner City Children* (Cambridge: Ballinger, 1975), pp. 69, 78.
20. Monk, pp. 179–80.
21. Ibid., p. 180.
22. Barth, *Run School Run*, pp. 86–87.
23. Monk, p. 172–73.
24. Ibid., p. 173. This conclusion was based on the principals' descriptions of teachers' conversations at school placement meetings.
25. Barth, *Run School Run*, p. 90.
26. Monk, pp. 172–73.

27. Highly recommended books offering suggestions on these and related topics are Jeannie Oakes and Martin Lipton, *Making the Best of Schools: A Handbook for Parents, Teachers, and Policymakers* (New Haven: Yale University Press, 1990); Roland S. Barth, *Improving Schools From Within: Teachers, Parents, and Principals Can Make the Difference* (San Francisco: Jossey-Bass, 1990); and William Rioux, *You Can Improve Your Child's School: Practical Answers to Questions Parents Ask Most About Their Public Schools* (New York: Simon and Schuster, 1980).

CHAPTER 9

1. Carnegie Council on Adolescent Development, *Turning Points: Preparing American Youth for the 21st Century* (Washington, D.C.: Carnegie Council on Adolescent Development, 1989).
2. R. D. Felner and A. M. Adan, "The School Transitional Environment Project: An Ecological Intervention and Evaluation," in R. H. Price et al., eds., *Fourteen Ounces of Prevention: A Casebook for Practitioners* (Washington, D.C.: American Psychological Association, 1988); R. D. Felner, M. Ginter, and J. Primavera, "Primary Prevention During School Transitions: Social Support and Environmental Structure," *American Journal of Community Psychology* 10 (1982): 277–90.
3. See Richard J. Murnane, Judith D. Singer, John B. Willett, James J. Kemple, and Randall J. Olsen, *Who Will Teach: Policies That Matter* (Cambridge: Harvard University Press, forthcoming, 1991), for compelling documentary and statistical evidence on the capacity of salary levels to attract and retain good teachers.
4. Union and management jointly devised a plan, including a grievance procedure, to meet this need in one school district, described in Richard J. Murnane, "Seniority Rules and Educational Productivity: Understanding the Consequences of a Mandate for Equality," *American Journal of Education* 90 (November 1981): 14–38.

Note: Page numbers followed by *n* indicate material in footnotes.

Absenteeism, 138, 147–149

Achievement: ad hoc policies and, 159–160; classroom membership and, 28–31, 81–82, 171–173, 209; effective schools research and, 99–103, 203; individual classroom experience and, 27–35, 75–92; prescriptive policies and, 113–115; school resources and, 20–28; socioeconomic status and, 23–24; student turnover and, 189–190; teaching methods and, 32

Ad hoc policies, 158–160

Alternative schools, 132–133, 135, 137, 151–152, 154, 156, 201

Alvarado, Anthony, 152

Analysis of variance, 20–21

Anticipation, 64–65

Assignment to classrooms, policies governing, 144, 145–147, 170–196

Attendance, policy for, 138, 144, 147–149

Authority, student challenges to, 56

Automated telephone calls to parents, 148

Averch, Harvey A., 34, 109–110

Barr, Rebecca, 13*n*, 22*n*

Barth, Roland, 175–177, 187–188, 190, 193

Berkeley, California, classroom assignment in, 172–175, 177

Berlin, Isaiah, 136
Berman, Paul, 110*n*, 115–122, 139*n*
Bilingual education, 9, 164–166
Black students. *See* Minority groups
Block classes, 162
Bonuses, 147
Brookover, Wilbur, 100

California Business Roundtable, 132*n*
Chall, Jeanne, 73
Change Agent study, 34, 116–122, 139
Chapter 1 program, 166–168
Classroom constitution, 40*n*
Classrooms: assignments to, 144, 145–147, 170–196; as basis of educational change, 207–209; changing of, by changing schools, 103–106; characteristics of, 40–49; choices among, 145, 153–157; effective schools research and, 101–103, 203; effect of treatment of others in, 40, 41–43; evolution of, 82–92; experiences of teachers in, 36–40; experimenting with, 201–203; impact of experiences in, 27–35; implementation of education policy and, 113–122; importance of daily life in, 1–2, 7; influence of schools on, 93–106; lengthy and sustained contact in, 40, 46–48, 53, 59; membership policies in, 76–82, 144–157, 170–196, 209;

mutual scrutiny in, 40, 43–46, 53; paying attention to, 199–200; policies to support, 157–163; relationship ideas in, 87–92; searching for solutions in, 85–87; shared vulnerability in, 84, 205; successful vs. unsuccessful, 34*n*; teacher and student choices in, 138–144; teacher and student roles in choosing, 140–144. *See also* Membership policies, classroom
Coleman, James S., 20–25, 33
Coleman report, 20–25, 33; studies following, 25–35
Comer, James, 160–161, 167
Control, metaphor of, 7–9
Cremin, Lawrence, 11
Critical mass classrooms, 161–162
Culture of the School and the Problem of Change, The (Sarason), 5*n*

Daily schedule, 162
Decentralizing effect of classrooms, 103
Dependency, of teachers and students in classrooms, 40–49, 53–55
Deregulation, 124–125, 126
Descriptive Analysis of Power, The (Nagel), 53*n*
Dickson, William, 26*n*
Dirigisme, 125
Domination, undermining classroom, 65–68

Dreeben, Robert, 13*n*, 22*n*
Dropouts, 201

East Harlem theme schools, 152
Education policy, 109–137; changing classrooms by changing schools in, 103–106; choices of teachers and students in, 138–144; classroom evolution and, 91–92; classroom experiences and, 27–35; classroom membership, 76–82, 144–157, 170–196; history of, 10–12; lessons of implementation for, 115–122; metaphor of control in, 7–9; metaphor of nurturance in, 7–9; reciprocal power and, 55–60, 71–74, 113–122. *See also* Laws of Education Policy; Membership policies, classroom; Pluralistic policies; Prescriptive policies
Education policy research: classroom differences in student achievement, 75–92; on effective schools, 99–103, 203; historic focus of, 2
Effective schools research, 99–103, 203
English immersion, 9, 164–166
Equality of Educational Opportunity (Coleman report), 20–25, 33
Evaluations, 2, 19, 25–26, 109–114, 202–203, 202*n*
Evolution of classrooms, 82–92
Expectations: changing, 104–105; effective schools research and, 99–103, 203; of students and teachers, 96–98
Experimental design evaluations, 202–203, 202*n*

Featherstone, Joseph, 5*n*
Federal government: education policy and, 111–112, 115–122; teacher policies of, 206
Federal Programs Supporting Educational Change (Change Agent study), 34, 116–122, 139
Feedback, 62–64
Fliegel, Sy, 152
Frames of Mind (Gardner), 87*n*, 88–89
Friedman, Milton, 126*n*

Gardner, Howard, 87*n*, 88–89
Goodlad, John, 61*n*
Greenberg, David, 153
Grether, David, 140

Hanushek, Eric, 12, 26–35, 113*n*
Hawthorne effect, 26
Head Start Planned Variation experiment, 120
High School in the Community, 162*n*
Hispanic students. *See* Minority groups
Home visits, 148

Homework, 90; classroom reciprocal power and, 71–74

Implementation: ad hoc, 165–166; of education policy, 115–122
Incentives, 123–126, 127
Instructional leaders, principals as, 100–102

Jackson, Philip W., 5n, 38

Laissez-faire, 124–125, 126
Laski, Harold, 136
Laws of Education Policy, 113, 121, 122, 142
Lezotte, Lawrence, 100
Life in Classrooms (Jackson), 5n, 38
Lightfoot, Sara Lawrence, 187
Lortie, Dan C., 5n
Los Angeles, student achievement study in, 30–31
Lukas, Carol VanDeusen, 120

Magnet schools, 132–133, 135, 137, 151–152, 154, 156, 201
Mann, Dale, 104, 161
Mayo, Elton, 26n
McCall, John, 153
McLaughlin, Milbrey Wallin, 104, 110n, 116–122, 139, 161
Meier, Deborah, 152

Membership policies, classroom, 76–82, 144–157, 170–196; assignment and reassignment, 144, 145–147, 170–196; attendance, 138, 144, 147–149; choices among schools and classrooms, 145, 153–157; recruiting, 144, 149–153; teacher and student roles in choosing, 140–144; turnover, 144, 148–149
Message centers, schools as, 94–99
Metaphor of control, 7–9
Metaphor of nurturance, 7–9
Mieszkowski, Peter, 140
Minigrants, 161
Minischools, 156
Minority groups: achievement of, 30–32; effective schools research and, 99–103; magnet schools and, 151–152; remedial instruction for, 166–168; reverse recruiting and, 152–153
Monk, David, 178–179, 181n, 182n, 183–184, 190, 193, 194
Mosteller, Frederick, 26, 33
Moynihan, Daniel Patrick, 26
Murnane, Richard, 30–32, 81, 128n, 140n, 142n
Mutual scrutiny, 40, 43–46, 53

Nagel, Jack H., 53n, 57n
National Board of Professional Teaching Standards, 92n
Neustadt, Richard E., 57n
New Haven, Connecticut, 162n

Newton Solution, 171–196, 208

New York City: East Harlem theme schools, 152

Nonprescriptive policies: deregulation, 124–125, 126; *dirigisme,* 125; incentives, 123–126, 127; laissez-faire, 124–125, 126; magnet schools, 132–133, 135, 137, 151–152, 154, 156, 201; special-interest programs, 132–133. *See also* Pluralistic policies

Nurturance, metaphor of, 7–9

Olsen, Randall, 140*n*

Olson, Lynn, 100*n*, 140*n*

On Equality of Educational Opportunity (Mosteller and Moynihan, eds.), 26

Opportunity cost, 140*n*

Parents, role in classroom assignment, 170–196

Place Called School, A (Goodlad), 61*n*

Pluralistic policies, 14, 126–137; classroom membership, 76–82, 144–157, 170–196; classroom support, 157–163; parts of, 126–127

Policy. *See* Education policy

Policy Effectiveness Hypothesis, 144

Power, 50–74; adjusting to other people's preferences and, 60–65; 79; defined, 50; shared vulnerability and, 53–55; of teachers and students to make choices, 140–144; undermining domination and, 65–68. *See also* Reciprocal power

Prescriptive policies, 110–115, 198; bilingual education, 9, 164–166; Chapter 1 program, 166–168; English immersion, 9, 164–166; improved existing, 163–169; school-based management, 16, 168–169

President's Commission on School Finance, 109–110

Prince Georges County, Maryland, 154

Principals, 105; classroom reciprocal power and, 158–163; of effective schools, 100–102; pluralistic policy and, 14; relationships with teachers, 129–135; role in classroom assignment, 172–196

Privacy, lack of classroom, 40, 43–46

Progressive education movement, 11

Pull-out classes, 166–168

Race: Coleman report and, 20–28; expectations and, 98

Rand Corporation, 115, 137

Random assignment research methods, 202–203, 202*n*

Ravitch, Diane, 111–112

Reassignment of students, 144, 146–147, 189–192

Reciprocal power, 55–60, 71–74, 140; in classroom evolution, 84–85; classroom membership and, 76–82; classroom reassignment and, 146–147; classroom support policies and, 158–163; described, 57–58; dispersal of, 58–60; effects on teaching and learning, 68–71; implementation of education policy and, 113–122; other people's preferences in, 60–65, 79; turnover and, 148–149, 156; undermining domination and, 65–68

Recruitment: of students, 144, 151–153, 201; of teachers, 144, 149–153, 156–157, 204–207

Remedial instruction, 146, 166–168

Research, improvements in, 202–203, 202*n*

Reverse recruiting, 152–153

Roethlisberger, Fritz, 26*n*

Romances, classroom, 45

Run School Run (Barth), 177

Salaries, of teachers, 147, 150, 201, 203, 204, 206

Sarason, Esther, 139

Sarason, Seymour B., 5*n*, 6, 40*n*, 67, 139

Schedule: changes in, 162; self-scheduling, 178

School-based management, 16, 168–169

Schools, 93–106; alternative or magnet, 132–133, 135, 137, 151–152, 154, 156, 201; changing classrooms by changing, 103–106; choices among, 145, 153–157; influence of, on teachers and parents, 93–99; research on effective, 99–103, 203; resources of, and achievement, 20–28; as sequences of classrooms, 94–99

Schoolteacher: A Sociological Study (Lortie), 5*n*

Self-scheduling, 178

Self-selection, 157; by teachers and students, 141–144

Shared vulnerability. *See* Vulnerability

Socioeconomic status, test scores and, 23–24

Special-interest programs, 132–133

State government: education policy and, 111–112; teacher policies of, 206

Students: ability to affect treatment of others in classroom, 40, 41–43, 53; assignment of, to classrooms, 144, 145–147, 170–196; attendance and, 138, 144, 147–149; changing expectations of, 104–105; classroom choices of, 138–144; classroom support policies and, 157–163; dropout, 201; experiences of, in classrooms, 36–40; impact of classroom experiences on, 6–7; implementation of education policy and, 113–122; importance of daily lives of, 3–6, 13–14; independence of, 2–3, 6; influence of schools on, 93–106; lengthy and sustained contact with teachers in, 40, 46–48, 53, 59; mutual scrutiny of teachers and, 40, 43–46, 53; power of, 50–53, 140–144; recruiting policy for, 144, 151–153, 156–157, 201; transmittal of information about, 94–99; turnover of, 148–149

Teacher conferences, 148
Teacher examinations, 91–92n
Teachers: ability to affect treatment of others in classroom, 40, 41–43, 53; assignment of, to classrooms, 144, 145–147; changing expectations of, 104–105; classroom choices of, 138–144; classroom support policies and, 157–163; effectiveness of, 31–35, 187–189, 203–207; effective schools research and, 101–103; experiences of, in classrooms, 36–40; implementation of education policy and, 113–122; importance of daily lives of, 3–6, 13–14; independence of, 2–3, 6; influence of schools on, 93–106; lengthy and sustained contact with students in, 40, 46–48, 53, 59; mutual scrutiny of students

and, 40, 43–46, 53; power of, 50–53, 140–144; recruiting policy for, 144, 149–153, 156–157, 204–207; relationships with principals, 129–135; role in classroom assignment, 172–196; salaries of, 147, 150, 201, 203, 204, 206; transmittal of information about, 94–99
Teachers' unions, 205
Testing, 19; Coleman report and, 20–28; in follow-up studies to Coleman report, 28–35; of teachers, 91–92n
Turnover, 144, 148–149, 156; classroom, 81–82; student achievement and, 189–190
Tyack, David, 10–11

Voluntary early retirement, 205
Vulnerability, 105–106; power and, 53–55; of teachers and students in classrooms, 40–49, 53–55

Weber, George, 100
Wise, Arthur, 112, 114–115
Wong, Clifford, 188